The Teaching of the English Language

BY

CHARLES CARPENTER FRIES

UNIVERSITY OF MICHIGAN

THOMAS NELSON AND SONS

NEW YORK

1927

Printed in United States of America

CONTENTS

PREFACE

THIS book attempts to discuss in a comprehensive way the problems that face the teacher who must deal with the "English" of pupils. It applies especially to the obligations of teachers of English, but it should also furnish the principles to guide any who seek to develop *good* English.

Even after more than a hundred years of linguistic study based upon the historical method, the fundamental principles upon which the modern scientific view of language rests and the results of scholarly investigations in the English language have not reached the schools. On the whole, the schools still perpetuate with very little change an eighteenth century point of view. The few attempts to popularize the scientific view and the results of scientific study have usually been in the nature of attacks upon the traditional ideas. This book is an effort to interpret the modern scientific view of language in a practical way for teachers. It presents not only a criticism of the older views and practices but also offers the principles of a constructive program and defines the objective of such teaching. It does not offer a detailed program for the study

PREFACE

of our language, for such a program could be adequately presented only in a series of school textbooks; it is concerned primarily with principles, but it is hoped that enough detail is furnished to point out clearly the path of such a detailed program.

For permission to reprint parts of an article which I formerly published under the title *What Is Good English?* I am grateful to *The English Journal;* and for a similar use of another article called *The Rules of the Common School Grammars,* I must thank Professor Carleton Brown, editor of the *Publications of the Modern Language Association.* The first appeared in *The English Journal* for November, 1925; the second in the *Publications of the Modern Language Association,* Volume XLII, pages 221-237.

CHAPTER I

THE RULES OF GRAMMAR AS THE MEASURE OF LANGUAGE ERRORS

FOR more than a century *good English* has been one of the major concerns of our educational system. To it as a study all pupils are required to give a large portion of their school time and it is the one required subject of the school curriculum that enjoys almost unanimous support from both the general community and the school authorities. These facts point to a definite consensus of opinion concerning the importance of acquiring what is considered a correct use of our mother tongue.

To match this almost unanimous opinion of the importance of *Good English,* however, there is the equally unanimous view that, despite the amount of time given to it, the schools have not succeeded in their teaching of the English language. The studies made of the "language errors" of school children and of college students seem to show a persistency of the same difficulties

1

throughout the grades and into the college and the university.[1]

Although there is general agreement in respect to the desirability of acquiring *good English* and also in respect to the view that the schools fail to teach it successfully, we do not by any means agree as to what this *good English* is. It is one of the recreations as well as one of the annoyances of English teachers to be continually bombarded with questions concerning correct forms, proper pronunciation, and the accurate use of words. The English teacher is asked time after time to decide bets made over disputed constructions, to recommend or supply authoritative manuals of correct English, and to *English* the papers of his colleagues. This question, "What is good English?" has not only the advantage of the keen interest of great numbers of people from all walks of life but also the disadvantages and difficulties arising from the fact that people seem to hesitate less in giving judgments with the

[1] See, for example, the summaries of such studies presented in the *Sixteenth Yearbook of the National Society for the Study of Education,* Part I, pp. 85-110, and in Stormzand and O'Shea, *How Much English Grammar?*

E. A. Cross, *Fundamentals in English,* pp. 425-446.

Other interesting studies of these facts are R. S. Johnson, *The Persistency of Errors in English Composition,* in *The School Review,* October, 1917.

S. A. Leonard, *How English Teachers Correct Papers,* in *English Journal* (October, 1923) Vol. XII, pp. 517-532.

tone of authority in matters of English language than in any other subject. More than that, the heat aroused over differences of opinion on points of English is equalled only by that generated by disputes upon questions of religion or of politics.

The first and also the most important popular point of view that one encounters who begins to deal with questions of grammatical correctness is the assumption that the rules of grammar as they are stated in our common school grammars are and must be the infallible measure of language errors. Some time ago the superintendent of schools of Cook County, Illinois, made a mildly liberal statement concerning several questions of English grammar. The material and the tone of the editorials which responded illustrate fairly this common view. The two examples given below express the attitude of the general public as well as that of most school teachers:

"The superintendent of schools for Cook County, Illinois, which includes so large a town as Chicago, has ruled that teachers and pupils under him may use 'he don't' and 'it is me' because these expressions in their correct form sound stilted and egotistical and are outlawed by common usage. With due regard for that official's judgment, it is safe to say that neither his nor any other man's similar verdict in such a case can escape the charge of provincialism. . . . Some better reason than a custom arising from ignorance, as seems to be the only excuse for the alterations in question, is needed for changing the English language. It would seem to be still the part of the schools to teach the language *strictly according to rule,* and to place emphasis on such teaching, rather than to encourage questionable liberties of usage." [2]

". . . And all this leads us . . . to the statement made by a Chicago school teacher a short time ago, in which the worthy scion of education expressed the opinion that constant usage has established such phrases as 'he don't,' 'I will' as a simple future tense, and 'it is me,' as correct. As a rule, we have not the reputation of being purist in our speech. . . . We may even make little errors ourselves now and then and we do not make the boast of the lady in the story who stated proudly, 'I ain't never made but one grammatical mistake, and I seen that one as soon as I done it.', . . . But we do stand out now and then for a few of the basic principles of grammar. If we make mistakes, they are unconscious, and we like to think they are not noticed, but it is our belief that when this Chicago educator attempts to overturn *the established rules of grammar* and to sneak in solecisms and flagrant errors under the guise of good usage, it is time to call a halt. . . . Errors of grammar . . . are inexcusable. If our speech is not necessarily pure, at least it can be correct, and we can avoid the use of expressions which we know—or at least, which we ought

[2] Boston, Feb. 23, 1921.

to know—to be *absolutely incorrect*. To an educated man, the use of 'he don't,' or of 'it is me'
grates just as much as 'I ain't' or 'I seen.' Any
teacher who would tell his pupils that the use of the
expressions, reported as countenanced by the Chicago educator, are in correct usage, is no fit person
to hold in his hand the education of growing boys
and girls of the United States."[3]

With these vigorous expressions should be compared one that comes from the seventeenth century.
It is concerned with the use of "you" when referring
to but one person. In the earlier stages of English
"thou," "thine," and "thee" were used when but
one person was addressed, and "ye," "your," "you,"
when speaking to more than one. By the end of the
sixteenth century the plural forms "you" or "ye"
became the pronouns for addressing politely but
one person; the old singular forms "thou" and
"thee" were ordinarily used only in addressing in-
feriors or those with whom the speaker was on very
intimate terms. The situation was similar to that
now existing in respect to the pronoun of the second
person in both German and French. After 1600 the
old singular forms of the pronoun of the second
person gradually disappeared and "you" became the
one form used in addressing all ranks of persons.
But this change was not effected without many pro-

[3] Ann Arbor, March 8, 1921.

tests. The reasoning and the tone of the one following deserves comparison with the attitude expressed in the editorials above. It is written by George Fox in 1660 and entitled "A Battle-Door for Teachers and Professors to learn Singular and Plural; *You* to Many, and *Thou* to One: Singular One, *Thou;* Plural Many, *You.*"

"Do not they speak false English, false Latine, false Greek . . . and false to the other Tongues, . . . that doth not speak *thou* to *one*, what ever he be, Father, Mother, King, or Judge; is he not a Novice and Unmannerly, and an Ideot and a Fool, that speaks *You* to *one*, which is not to be spoken to a *singular*, but to *many?* O Vulgar Professors and Teachers, that speaks Plural when they should Singular. . . . Come you Priests and Professors, have you not learnt your Accidence?"

Very generally is it taken for granted that only that language is correct which is "strictly according to rule." The rules of our common school grammars are accepted as an adequate measure of right and wrong, and "correctness" according to this standard is considered by many the first requisite of good English.

In accord with this point of view "It is me" is condemned as wrong because the form "me" violates the rule that "the verb 'to be' takes the same case after it as stands before it." "He had wrote" is likewise judged to be incorrect grammar because of the rule that "with the auxiliary 'have' or 'had' the past participle must be used, not the form of the simple past tense." And "Has everyone handed in their papers?" is held to be an error because it conflicts with the rule that "a pronoun agrees with its antecedent in number." This attitude that the conventional rules are the measure of correct English underlies the common grammatical ideas of most people and is the assumption upon which is based much of the educational investigation of the language errors of school children.[4] It therefore deserves the most serious consideration.

In such a situation the historical method of approach promises the most light. We shall be in a better position to evaluate the present views if we understand the origin and nature of these ideas and rules of language which have been so deeply rooted in popular prejudice.

The immediate source of the common grammatical ideas and ideals of today is the nineteenth century school grammars. Of these, Lindley Murray's *English Grammar* was by far the most extensively used in the schools of both England and America. First published in 1795 it ran through, in

---

[4] See the studies referred to in note No. 1. According to these studies these three rules of grammar are most frequently violated.

its various forms, more than two hundred editions during the nineteenth century. It is with some justice, therefore, that Lindley Murray is looked upon as the "father" of our school grammars. But Lindley Murray does not pretend to make an original contribution. His work is a compilation (to use his own term) of the grammars that were prominent during the latter half of the eighteenth century.[5] If one judges influence by the number of editions published and by the frequency with which the books are quoted or copied there seems to be little doubt that the outstanding grammars of the second half of the eighteenth century were Robert Lowth's *A Short Introduction to English Grammar* (1762), William Ward's *A Grammar of the English Language* (1765), and Charles Coote's *Elements of the Grammar of the English Language* (1788).

These grammars are important for our consideration not only as the source of Lindley Murray's grammatical materials but also because they were the grammars first introduced into the schools as the demand for the teaching of English became insistent and partly successful toward the end of the

[5] See the *Introduction*, Lindley Murray's *English Grammar*, (1795). The pertinent parts of the documents which furnish the evidence for the statements made throughout the remainder of this chapter are printed in my study *The Rules of the Common School Grammars*, in the *Publications of the Modern Language Association*, Vol. XLII, March, 1927.

eighteenth century. As early as 1581 Mulcaster, in his labored discussion of what seemed to him to be the fundamental problems of teaching, argued for increased attention to the study of the English language.[6] But it was not until more than (two hundred years later,) after the demands for the teaching of English had become not only more frequent but decidedly more vigorous, that the study of English in the form of English grammar became part of the accepted curriculum of the schools. Thus through the schools the grammars of Lowth (1762), Ward (1765), and Coote (1788), together with the contemporary dictionaries of Johnson, Sheridan, and Walker, set the ideas of language and grammar that dominated Lindley Murray and the nineteenth century school texts.

It is essential, therefore, to understand the purposes and the views of language which were held by these grammarians and dictionary makers. They have themselves furnished us with the material we need, for the prefaces and introductions to their books contain many frank and enlightening statements of their attitudes toward their work. We shall attempt to summarize the significant features of their views and then to see these views in relation to the important circumstances of the times in which they were developed and expressed.

[6] Richard Mulcaster, *Positions,* (1581) p. 30.

The purposes of the leading grammarians of the eighteenth century differed fundamentally from those of the writers of the English grammars of the preceding hundred years. Most of the grammars published from 1586, the date of the first English grammar,[7] to the end of the seventeenth century were of two kinds. They were either directed to foreigners who wished to learn English and for this purpose were often written in Latin or in French; or they were quite frankly introductions to the study of Latin, and aimed simply to take advantage of the use of the pupil's native language in order to facilitate his mastery of Latin grammar. The grammars of the eighteenth century, however, were usually English grammars for English people. They aimed to teach English people correct English. The authors of this group of grammars are in somewhat surprising agreement in their expression of either or both of the following purposes: (a) to reduce the language to rule, to "churn it into method"; and (b) to correct the usage of English people by making it conform to a standard of "reason."

Some typical statements of these purposes, chosen from many of a similar nature, are the following:

"I cannot but think it would be of great Advantage, both for the Improvement of Reason in gen-

---

[7] W. Bullokar, *Brej Grammar,* (1586).

eral (the Art of Speaking having such an Affinity with that of Reasoning, which it represents) and also for the exact use of our own Language; which for want of Rule is subject to Uncertainty, and the Occasion of frequent Contentions. And upon this account, it has been the Practice of several wise Nations, such of them, I mean, as have a thorough Education, to learn even their own Language by Stated Rules, to avoid that Confusion, that must needs follow from leaving it wholly to vulgar Use. Sure no Body need think long upon this Subject to be convinced, that if there go so much Art to right reasoning, there must go some also to right speaking, I mean to a clear and certain Expression of that Reason, which is the Business of Grammar. Certainly Chance can never equal Rule and Method in a thing of this Moment and Curiosity. The Subject therefore of this Treatise, is no matter of little Concernment, by which so much Good may be done in the World." [8]

". . . these [naming several grammarians] deserved well of their Country, for their laudable Endeavours to cultivate and improve their own Native Speech, which has long lain, and is at this Day too much neglected, notwithstanding the many brave, but unsuccessful Attempts, to bring it into request, by reducing it to order, and shewing the Beauties and Excellencies it is capable of." [9]

[8] Richard Johnson, *Grammatical Commentaries*, **(1706)** Preface.
[9] Anon. *A New English Accidence*, (1736) Preface.

"Thus have I laboured to settle the orthography, to regulate the structures, and ascertain the signification of English words." [10]

"Whether many important advantages would not accrue both to the present age, and to posterity, if the English language were ascertained, and reduced to a fixed and permanent standard? . . . To compass these points . . . has been the chief object of the author's pursuits in life, and the main end of the present publication." [11]

"Considering the many grammatical Improprieties to be found in our best Writers, such as Swift, Addison, Pope &c. a Systematical English Syntax is not beneath the Notice of the Learned themselves." [12]

("The principal design of a Grammar in any Language is to teach us to express ourselves with propriety in that Language, and to enable us to judge of every phrase and form of construction whether it be right or not.) The plain way of doing this, is to lay down rules, and to illustrate them by examples.) But, besides shewing what is right, the matter may be further explained by pointing out what is wrong." [13]

[10] Samuel Johnson, Preface to Grammar and Dictionary, (1755).

[11] Thomas Sheridan, Preface to Dictionary, (1780).

[12] James Buchanan, *A Regular English Syntax*, (1767) Preface vi.

[13] Robert Lowth, *A Short Introduction*, etc. (1762) Preface, x.

" . . . it is manifest that some Rules for the Construction of the Language must be used, and those
Rules reduced to some Kind of System. . . . Thus
I have given in Effect, and with its principal Difficulties, the whole Plan of a Speculative or Theoretic
Grammar, with regard to the English Language . . .
to attempt a Discovery of the Reason of every Part
of Construction. . . . Hence Use and Custom are
con sidered as the only Rules by which to judge of
what is right or wrong in Process. But is the Custom which is observed in the Application of any
Language the Effect of Chance? Is not such a
Custom a consistent Plan of communicating the
Conceptions and rational discursive Operations of
one Man to another? And who will maintain, that
this is, or can be, the Effect of unmeaning Accident?
If then it be not so, it must be the Effect of the
Reason of Man, adjusting certain means to a certain
End: And it is the Business of Speculative or Rational Grammar to explain the Nature of the Means,
and to shew how they are applied to accomplish the
End proposed. If this can be done with sufficient
Evidence, the most simple of the Elements of Logic
will become familiar to those who engage in a
Course of Grammar, and Reason will go Hand in
Hand with Practice." [14]

In the attempt of the eighteenth century grammarians to reduce the language to rule and to purge
it of its "crudities" they definitely repudiated usage,
even the usage of the best authors, as the standard

[14] William Ward, *English Grammar,* (1765) Preface, v, xvii, xxi.

of correctness. The attitude of these grammarians
was not simply a *limitation* of the usage to be observed as it was for Ben Jonson.

" . . . yet when I name custom, I understand not
the vulgar custom; for that were a precept no less
dangerous to language than to life, if we should
speak or live after the manners of the vulgar: but
that I call custom of speech, which is the consent of
the learned; as custom of life, which is the consent
of the good." [15]

For these eighteenth century grammarians, however, *no* usage or "custom," not even that of the
"learned," was accepted as a basis for grammatical
correctness. Statements from the grammars are
abundant. I quote four typical expressions of this
attitude from those eighteenth century books shown
above to be of especial importance in determining
the materials of our nineteenth century school
grammars.

"But let us consider, how, and in what extent, we
are to understand this charge brought against the
English Language. [Referring to Swift's statement
that our language *offends against every part of
grammar*]. . . . Does it mean that the English
Language, as it is spoken by the politest part of the
nation, and as it stands in the writings of our most
approved authors, often offends against every part

[15] Ben Jonson, *Discoveries*, No. 129. (Quoting Quintilian).

of grammar? Thus far, I am afraid, the charge is true." [16]

"This piece [referring to the work of Lowth] is excellent on account of the Notes, in which are shewn the grammatic Inaccuracies that have escaped the Pens of our most distinguished Writers. . . . If your Scholars are Natives of England . . . false English pointed out to them may be of the greatest Use; For they are apt to follow Custom and example, even where it is faulty, till they are apprized of their Mistake: And therefore by shewing where Custom is erroneous, his Lordship has well deserved the Thanks of everyone who values the English Language and Literature. . . . In short, a very blamable Neglect of grammatic Propriety has prevailed amongst the English Writers, and at length we seem to be growing generally sensible of it; as likewise of the Use which may be made of a Knowledge of the English Grammar, towards assisting Children to comprehend the general Import and Advantage of Rules concerning Language." [17]

" . . . yet so little regard has been paid to it [the English language] . . . that out of our numerous array of authors, very few can be selected who write with accuracy; . . . Nay it has lately been proved by a learned Prelate in an essay upon our grammar, that some of our most celebrated writers, and such as have hitherto passed for our English

[16] Robert Lowth, *A Short Introduction,* etc., (1762).
[17] William Ward, *English Grammar,* (1765).

classics, have been guilty of great solecisms, inaccuracies, and even grammatical improprieties, in
many places of their most finished works." [18]

"Among the middling ranks of life, grammar appears to be too much disregarded. . . .
"The members of the three learned professions are
confessedly superior to the generality in the accurate use of their native language. But even among
them, there is some deficiency in this respect. . . .
"Persons of rank and fashion, though they generally speak with ease and elegance, are not remark-
able for being models of accurate expression.
"Authors are, without controversy, the persons on
whom it is more particularly incumbent both in
speaking and writing, to observe a strict adherence
to grammatical propriety. . . . But this is a point
to which the greater part even of our most esteemed
writers have not sufficiently attended.
"This deficiency in grammatical precision may
be obviated and supplied by a competent degree of
attention, in the first place, to the fundamental
principles of grammar, and, secondly to the particu-   .
lar rules of the language." [19]

In other words the grammarians here assume a
certain accurate, absolute measuring rod of correc-
tions in grammar, and repudiate all usage that does
not conform to this standard. Such "incorrect"

[18] Thomas Sheridan, Preface to his *Dictionary*, (1780).
[19] Charles Coote, *English Grammar*, (1788).

language is to be found among all classes of men, even in the "most polished writings" **of our** "most approved authors." It is the "doctrine of original sin" in grammar. From this point of view any construction contrary to this arbitrary standard of rules, no matter how much or whose usage supports it, will still remain false or bad grammar. The attitude here expressed is not simply the recognition of *a standard* but that particular kind of linguistic purism which, in making a standard, ignores practice and sets up theoretical reasoning as the guide.

There were two writers of grammars (Priestley (1761) and Webster (1789) who protested—in theory at least—against the general tendency of the grammarians toward arbitrary rules and the repudiating of usage. Their voices, however, were not heeded and their point of view was not that of the predominating grammars of the latter part of the eighteenth century and of the nineteenth century.

Whence, then, did these eighteenth century grammarians derive their measures of "correct" language? The rules furnished in the grammars were generally either carried over from Latin syntax or the new creations of a so-called "rational grammar" and thus based upon "reason" or the "laws of thought." An example of the latter type of rules are those concerning the "correct" use of *shall* and *will,* then

first developed in all their intricacies.[20]   The following is a frank expression of the use of the rules
of the Latin grammars.

"Considering the many grammatical Improprieties to be found in our best Writers, such as Swift,
Addison, Pope, etc. a Systematical English Syntax
is not beneath the Notice of the Learned themselves.
Should it be urged, that in the Time of these
Writers, English was but a very little subjected to
Grammar, that they had scarcely a single Rule to
direct them, a question readily occurs: Had they not
the Rules of Latin Syntax to direct them?" [21]

Despite the fact that some of the grammarians
recognize the fact that the apparatus of the Latin
grammars is not suitable for the treatment of the
English language they all use it,[22] fearing to intro-

[20] See C. C. Fries, *The Periphrastic Future with Shall and Will
in Modern English,* in *Publications of the Modern Language
Association,* XL, pp. 967-983.

[21] James Buchanan, *English Grammar,* Preface.

[22] For the beginnings of the grammatical apparatus used in the
early English grammars one must turn back to the classical
Greece of the fourth and even the fifth century before the
Christian era—to the names of Protagoras and Prodicus, Democri-
tus and Aristotle, the Stoics and the Alexandrian critics. In
the second century B. C. there existed two hostile schools of
Greek grammarians: (a) the "Analogists" insisted, first, that
there was a strict law of analogy between the word and the
idea for which it stood, and, second, that there could be no
exceptions to the grammatical rules they laid down; (b) the
"Anomalists" opposed the "Analogists" by denying that there

duce innovations and also desiring to lay a good foundation for the learning of Latin while teaching English grammar.

---

was any necessary connection between the word and the idea and they insisted that there could be no grammatical rules of any kind except in so far as they were consecrated by custom.

The outstanding figure of the "Anomalists" was Crates of Mallos who produced the first Greek grammar, a collection of facts gathered by the Alexandrian critics in their minute study of the differences between the language of Homer and the Attic writers and that of their own day. The immediate cause of Crates' grammar was his lectures at Rome on the comparison of the Greek and Latin languages, delivered during his residence there as an official representative of his country. -

Of the "Analogists," Aristarchus stood out as the most important figure. Dionysius Thrax was the pupil of Aristarchus, so that his famous grammar, published in the time of Pompey when the Romans were zealously studying Greek, assumed as a foundation the principles of the Analogist school of grammarians. Upon this grammar of Dionysius Thrax were modelled the Latin grammars of Rome which attempted (with only partial success) to translate into Latin the Greek technical grammatical terms.

By the second century of the Christian era the Anomalist school of grammarians had virtually no influence upon the making of Latin grammars and the Analogists had thus practically won the dispute. In the books of grammar that were being produced "analogy" was recognized as the principle underlying language although the "rules" were acknowledged to have some exceptions. One outstanding name of those who wrote Latin grammars modelled upon that of Dionysius Thrax and the Latin grammars that followed his is that of Donatus of the (fourth century A. D.)

Upon the grammar of Donatus and the work of Priscian, of about (500 A. D.), were based the grammars of the Middle Ages. These are the type and source of the Latin and Greek grammars of Medieval and Modern Europe. The grammatical

"It must indeed be acknowledged that the *Plan of the Latin Grammar,* is not the best which might be contrived, especially for our English youth, but as Custom and Authority have made it the Standard Rule for teaching them that Language, there seems therefore a necessity of making the Rules of an Introduction to an English Grammar, as subservient thereunto as possible, . . . that whilst we are teaching the one, we may at the same time be laying a good Foundation for the other." [23]

This, then, is the grammatical material and the language point of view that has been rehearsed and repeated in the school grammars of the past century with surprisingly little change. To appreciate its significance one must attempt to see it with some completeness against the background of the circumstances attending its rise and development.

---

apparatus developed and available in the sixteenth century when the first practical grammars of the vernaculars arose was this, which had been used for centuries for the Latin language—it is the dead hand of the old Analogist group of the second century B. C.)

It is to be remembered that the fundamental ideas of this school of grammarians were opposed from the very beginning even with reference to the classical languages themselves. Present scientific views of language are more in harmony with the point of view of the old Anomalists than with that of the Analogists and their descendants.

See Sayce, article on *Grammar,* Encyclopædia Britannica, 11th edition; Jespersen, *Language,* pp. 19-26; Croce, *Æsthetic,* (trans. Ainslie), pp. 464-466.

[23] Anon., *A New English Accidence,* (1736).

Many have pointed out that the search for "correctness" in language attended the rise of the middle classes into social prominence during the eighteenth century.[24] There are, however, other factors which contributed to the building of the language ideas and ideals of the time. There are two which seem to me to bear directly upon the views expressed by the grammarians.

The first is the attitude toward the English language as it developed through the sixteenth, seventeenth, and early eighteenth centuries. Up to and indeed during the first half of the sixteenth century the vernaculars—Italian, French, Spanish, as well as English—were discredited when compared with the classical languages. Not only was this disrespect the point of view of learning and the schools but also to a great extent the attitude of writers. The charge most frequently made was that of poverty of words and resulting inability to express in English the shades of meaning of which Latin was capable.[25] As a result, many—William Caxton among the first—set out to enrich the English vo-

[24] Henry Cecil Wyld, *History of Modern Colloquial English*, p. 18.

[25] Tyndale, in 1528, found it necessary to contend for the use English in the translating of his New Testament.

"St. Jerome translated the Bible into his mother-tongue why maye not we also! They will say it cannot be translated into our tongue, it is so rude. It is not so rude as they are false lyers." Skeat, *Specimens*, p. 172.

cabulary by importing Latin words with little change of form.

With the growth of literature in English toward the end of the reign of Queen Elizabeth less is heard of reproach for the English language on the score of poverty of vocabulary. The resources of English are recognized and praised, but there is frequently expressed the feeling that the English language is a "rude" tongue, a wild growth needing to be definitely "pruned" or corrected. It is this attitude which expressed itself in the growing demand for an authoritative purging of the language of its improprieties and the setting up of a definite standard by which to measure its accuracy. In Italy and in France academies for this purpose [26] were established early.[27]   In England, in spite of a series of proposals [28] for the setting up of such an academy "to

[26] "La principale fonction de l' Académie sera de travailler avec tout le soin et toute la diligence possible à donner des règles certaines à notre langue, et à la rendre pure, éloquente et capable de traiter les arts et les sciences."
Statutes of Foundation of French Academy, Article No. 24, Ferdinand Brunot, *Histoire de la Langue Française,* Tome III, 35.

[27] The Florentine Academy dated from 1542.
The Academia della Crusca was founded in 1582.
The Salon de Rambouillet received the official sanction of Richelieu in 1635.

[28] Some of the expressions of desire for an English Academy came from the following: Edmund Bolton, 1617; John Dryden, 1664, 1679; John Evelyn, 1665; S. Skinner, 1671; Defoe, 1697; Addison, 1711; Swift, 1712.

correct and fix" the English language, no authorized academy was established. During the century in which the proposal was advocated probably Swift's well-known letter to the lord treasurer (Harley, Earl of Oxford) was the most vigorous pleading for such a body and marked the time when the plan came nearest to receiving royal sanction. He says:

"My lord, I do here, in the name of all the learned and polite persons of the nation complain to your lordship, . . . that our language is extremely imperfect: that its daily improvements are by no means in proportion to its daily corruptions: that the pretenders to polish and refine it, have chiefly multiplied abuses and absurdities; and that in many instances it offends against every part of grammar . . . and these corruptions very few of the best authors in our age have wholly escaped. . . .

"They all agreed, that nothing would be of greater use . . . than some effectual method for correcting, enlarging, and ascertaining our language; and they think it a work very possible to be compassed under the protection of a prince, the countenance and encouragement of a ministry, and the care of proper persons chosen for such an undertaking."

Although there were still echoes of these proposals for a half century after the passing of Queen Anne, it was with the coming of the Hanoverians in 1714 that hope of imitating the French Academy van-i hed. These efforts to create an "academy" in England failed. No authoritative body was created for the purpose of providing a definite standard for the English language, to "prune it of its crudities" and its "false syntax" and to "bring it into methods." But instead of such an academy, recognized for this purpose, there were published after the first quarter of the eighteenth century an increasing number of English grammars whose authors (as we have seen above) definitely set out to do for the language this very "reducing to rule," this "churning into method" which it was hoped an academy would accomplish. Indeed the grammars that came after 1750 actually did fulfill for the English language the purposes of an Academy, furnishing a definite standard of correctness and propriety.

The other element in the background against which one should view the attitudes of the grammarians of the second half of the eighteenth century is the expression of standards of literary criticism of this time and of the preceding age. Without entering the discussion concerning the relative importance of the various critical creeds and theories of literature and art in the point of view of the eighteenth century, one can, from undisputed materials safely conclude that neo-classicism did exist and that there was much discussion of "rules" and 'reason" and "correct writers." Vaughan sums up the essential elements of the "Neo-classic creed" in discussing Samuel Johnson as a critic. "This method," he says, "takes for granted certain fixed laws—whether the laws formulated by Aristotle, or by Horace, or the French critics, is for the moment beside the question—and passes sentence on every work of art according as it conforms to the critical decalog or transgresses it."

And again, "Throughout, he [Johnson] assumes that the principles of art . . . are fixed and invariable. To him they form a kind of case-law, which is to be extracted by the learned from the works of a certain number of 'correct writers,' ancient and modern, and which, once established, is binding for all time on the critic and on those he summons to his bar."

Whatever importance this critical attitude may have held in the general view of literary criticism throughout the first half of the eighteenth century, it was repudiated and supplanted by romantic criticism and the historical method by the end of that century. But in the narrower field of language as it was viewed in the grammars and taught in the schools this neo-classic creed of "rules" as the measure of "correctness" has had a vigorous existence and still continues to dominate the popular standards of judgment. Our common school grammars

even yet rest in large measure upon this eighteenth
century ideal and have appropriated surprisingly
little of the results of the last hundred years of
linguistic scholarship based upon the historical
method.

A brief summary will serve to point more clearly
the relation of the facts here presented. The pleading for an academy in English as established in
France, beginning in the seventeenth century and
expressed with considerable vigor in the early part
of the eighteenth century, was not successful. But
instead of such an academy recognized for the purpose of providing a definite standard of correctness
for the English language there were published in
the second and third quarters of the eighteenth century an increasing number of English grammars
whose authors definitely set out to do for the language those very things which it was hoped an
academy would accomplish. The standard of correctness and propriety furnished by these grammars
was not based upon usage, for the grammarians
insisted that "even our most approved authors
offended against every part of grammar"; but it
was a standard based upon Latin syntax and "reason" and expressed in arbitrary rules. The grammars originating in this attitude exerted also
something of an authoritative influence over the
language (especially over that of succeeding gen-

erations), for it was these grammars that supplied the demand for the teaching of English in the schools toward the end of the eighteenth century, and they were the sources of Lindley Murray's grammar and the school texts of the nineteenth century. Deeply rooted in this way through the schools, the ideas of language, the grammar conventions, the standards of correctness, have been rehearsed and repeated so that the common grammatical ideas and ideals of today preserve with but little damage the eighteenth-century "academy." This linguistic attitude, expressing itself in grammars of arbitrary rules seems to be but another manifestation and survival of that tendency called the neo-classic creed of literary criticism.

The historical method in language which began with the opening of the nineteenth century, and upon which modern linguistic scholarship rests has had practically no effect upon school teachers generally and the makers of the common school grammars. In order the more definitely to test the rules as the final measure of correctness let us examine historically the particular examples given above.

Although we condemn "It is me" as violating the rule for case following the verb "to be," we all of us accept "It is you" as perfectly good English. A historical view of the inflections of the personal pronouns of the first and second person reveals the following situation:

FIRST PERSON

Old English forms		Modern English
Nom.	ic	*These become in*	I
Gen.	mīn		(mine) my
Dat.	mē		me
Acc.	(mec) mē		me

SECOND PERSON

Old English forms		Modern English
Nom.	gē	*These become in*	ye
Gen.	ēower		your
Dat.	ēow		you
Acc.	(ēowic) ēow		you

Historically, "It is me" uses precisely the same case-form as "It is you." "Me" and "you" were both dative-accusative forms in Old English. In respect to the pronoun of the second person, however, "you" gradually displaced "ye" in some situations and then "ye" disappeared from common use. "You," the old dative-accusative form, is now accepted in "It is you" solely because we use it in that situation. If, then, "It is me" is to be condemned as incorrect grammar the only sound basis for that decision must be that we do not use "me" in this expression. Obviously the rule that "the verb 'to be' takes the same case after it as is used before it" is not the final measure to be applied in this case but must yield, as rules have always done, to the drift and development of the language.[29]

As we turn to examine, in similar fashion, "He had wrote," let me insist, in order to avoid possible misunderstanding, that I am not now giving judgment concerning the correctness or acceptability of the examples I am using. I am simply trying to examine critically the standards by which this correctness is usually measured. Although we condemn "He had wrote," we do accept "The sun had shone," or "He has stood there for ten minutes." Historically, however, "write" and "shine" belong to the same class of verbs. The principal parts of these three verbs in Old English were:

Present Infinitive	Preterit or Past Tense (Singular)	Past Participle
wrītan	wrāt	writen
scīnan	scān	scinen
standan	stōd	standan

From the historical point of view, "shone," "stood," and "wrote," all three, are the forms of the simple past tense. If the rule quoted above is indeed the valid measure of correctness, then we ought to say "The sun has 'shinnen,'" and "He has 'standen' there ten minutes." If "had wrote" is incorrect and

[29] The *c'est moi* of the French is a parallel expression; no Frenchman would say *c'est je.*

"has stood" is correct all that can be urged as the reason for the decision is that we use the one but do not use the other. There are many verbs in which we thus use with the auxiliary the forms that are historically the simple past tense forms. If, in objection, one asserts that the past participle of "shine" is now "shone" and that of "stand" is now "stood," then in like process if we habitually use "wrote" rather than the form "written" with "have" or "had," then the form "wrote" will be called the new past participle of the verb "write." In other words, the rule insists that "with the auxiliary 'have' or 'had' must be used the past participle," and then we define as the past participle whatever form of the verb is used with the "have" or "had." Can such a circle lead to insight into language?

When then one brings together into a single view the facts of the circumstances under which the conventional rules of grammar were framed and accepted, together with the facts of the historical development of the English language, he is driven to conclude that these rules are not a safe and complete guide to correctness in English grammar.

SELECTED REFERENCES

BRYAN, W. F., *Notes on the Founders of Prescriptive English Grammar*, in *Manly, Anniversary Studies*, pp. 383-393.

BRYAN, W. F., *A Late Eighteenth Century Purist*, in *Studies in Philology*, July, 1926, Vol. XXIII.

CROCE, BENEDETTO, *Æsthetic*, (trans. Ainslie, 1922). Pp. 142-152; 172-174; 209-210; 225-226; 324-333; 401-402; 464-466.

FRIES, C. C., *The Rules of the Common School Grammars*, in *Publications of the Modern Language Association*, March, 1927. Vol. XLII.

JESPERSEN, OTTO, *Language; Its Nature, Development, and Origin*, Book I.

Encyclopædia Britannica, 11th edition, *Grammar*.

Encyclopædia of Education, *Grammar (English)*.

CHAPTER II

Standards of Acceptable English: Grammar

If, then, the conventional rules of our common school grammars do not furnish a valid guide to correct grammar where can we look for the standards of acceptable English? As has already been hinted in the discussion of the examples used in the preceding chapter, the only grammatical correctness there can be in English (or in language generally) must rest on usage. Where that usage is practically unanimous,[1] as it is in respect to "It

---

[1] The following statement indicates the amount of emphasis which must be put upon the word *practically* when language usage is described as *unanimous*.

"Every one knows that language is variable. Two individuals of the same generation and locality, speaking precisely the same dialect and moving in the same social circles, are never absolutely at one in their speech habits. A minute investigation of the speech of each individual would reveal countless differences of detail—in choice of words, in sentence structure, in the relative frequency with which particular forms or combinations of words are used, in the pronunciation of particular vowels and consonants and of combinations of vowels and consonants, in all those features, such as speed, stress, and tone, that give life to spoken language. In a sense they speak slightly divergent dialects of the same language rather than identically the same language. . . . If all the speakers of a given dialect were

is you," there is no possible appeal despite any
rules that may come into conflict with it. In such
cases, if the rule of grammar does not harmonize
with the general usage of the language it has no
validity. Rules or laws of grammar are like laws
of botany, or physics, or biology; they are general
statements attempting to describe the ways in which
language operates to express ideas, and valid only
in so far as they are accurate generalizations. But
the facts of usage are in all cases fundamental. If
these facts are not in harmony with the rules or
generalizations we have had in our grammars
hitherto, then these rules must be restated and ex-
panded to include all the facts. There can thus
never be in grammar an error that is both very

---

arranged in order in accordance with the degree of their conformity to average usage, there is little doubt that they would
constitute a very finely intergrading series clustered about a
well-defined norm. The differences between any two neighboring
speakers of the series (this does not refer in any way to those
with marked speech defects nor to foreigners who have acquired the language late in life) would be negligible for any
but the most microscopic research. The differences between
the outermost members of the series are sure to be considerable,
in all likelihood considerable enough to measure up to a true
dialect variation. What prevents us from saying that these
untypical individuals speak distinct dialects is that their peculiarities, as a unified whole, are not referable to another norm
than the norm of their own series."

Edward Sapir, *Language,* pp. 157, 158, 159.

bad and very common. The more common it is, the nearer it comes to being the best of grammar.

But difficulties do not arise in cases where the usage is fairly unanimous. "It is you" is not a problem; but with the pronoun of the first person there is a problem because some people insist upon using "It is I," and others "It is me." The trouble arises where usage is thus divided, in those cases in which adult English-speaking people differ in their practice. Here, obviously, the appeal to usage is futile because it is the very fact of the division of usage which creates the difficulty. Some would suggest that the practice of the educated group should determine the judgment. This suggestion would be quite satisfactory were it not for two things: there are divisions of usage among the educated themselves; and, more important still, no one has ever given us a satisfactory measuring rod by which we can decide whether any particular person belongs to this educated group or not. Those who offer the suggestion frequently make the language one uses the standard by which to judge one's education. The suggestion, in practice, usually turns out as follows. We agree to let the usage of the educated decide whether "It is me" is acceptable, and then when we offer examples from the language of Smith, Jones, or Brown, who habitually use "It is me," it is insisted that because Smith, Jones, and Brown use "It is me" (or similar constructions) they cannot be included in the group of the educated.

It is probably much more sound to decide that the spontaneous usage of that large group who are carrying on the affairs of English-speaking people is the usage to be observed and to set the standard. Certainly this would seem sound as far as the teaching of the schools is concerned if we agree that education must bear directly upon and prepare for life.[2] When, then, this usage is practically unanimous in respect to any form or construction that form or construction is correct and acceptable English grammar. When this usage differs in respect to any form or construction we must set up some other principle of decision. To do that is the purpose of the rest of this chapter.

Toward this end let us examine the third of the examples given in the preceding chapter. "Has everyone handed in their papers?" is condemned as incorrect grammar because it violates the rule that "a pronoun agrees with its antecedent in number." Two other rules should be considered in connection

[2] To avoid possible misunderstanding let me call attention to the fact that we are not here discussing the artistic use of language nor are we attempting to define any ideal of the highest reaches of our language in beauty and effectiveness. We are here trying to outline some practical standards of *acceptable* English. The artistic point of view will be discussed in Chapter V and the significance of differing speech habits in the various groups will be dealt with in Chapter VI.

with this one. I quote them as they are stated in the Kirby Grammar Test: (IV, e.) "The verb should agree in number with the subject" and (V, g.) "An adjective agrees in number with the noun it modifies." These, the usual rules concerning agreement in number, are the measures by which many cases of pupil usage, and of newspaper usage, and of teacher usage, and of writer usage are judged to be incorrect.

Just what does agreement or concord mean? The analysis of the forms of inflection in the two sentences following as these sentences are rendered in Latin, Greek, and Old English will help make clear the significance of the rules for agreement.

	A.	B.
Mdn.E.	The good man wrote.	The good men wrote.
Latin.	Bonus homo scripsit.	Boni homines scripsērunt.
Greek.	ὁ ἀγαθὸς ἄνθρωπος ἔγραψε.	οἱ ἀγαθοὶ ἄνθρωποι ἔγραψαν.
Old.E.	Sē gōda mann wrāt.	þā gōdan menn writon

In the sentences in column A the subject noun "man" is singular. There is but one man who wrote. In the Latin sentence the form of the noun tells us that there is but one man; it says singular number. But the ending of the adjective *-us* and the ending of the verb *-it* both repeat the information that there is but one man; they are both singular number. In the Greek rendering not only do the adjective and the verb repeat the information conveyed by the form of the noun as to the number but the form of the article also adds its voice to the chorus that shouts singular. So, too, in Old English each of the four words by its form conveys the same bit of information, that there is but one man. In the sentences in the B column the subject noun is plural, "men." In the Latin sentence this plurality of the subject is told us three times: in adjective, in noun, and in verb. In the Greek, as well as in the Old English sentence it is indicated four times: in article, in adjective, in noun, and in verb. Agreement or concord in number means that the singular or plural number of the noun is indicated not only by the form of the noun itself, but also by the grammatical forms of other words; it means that this single piece of information concerning the noun is conveyed several times. In the Latin sentences both the adjective and the verb thus agree with the subject in number. In the Greek and the Old English sentences the adjective, the verb, and the article all three agree with the subject in number.

But in the Modern English sentences, do the forms of either the adjective or the verb show in any way the number of the noun with which they are said to agree? Is it true that the adjective "good" agrees with the nouns "man" or "men" in number? Why not also insist that the article "the" agrees with the noun in number? These words, the article "the," the adjective "good," the verb "wrote," are exactly the same whether the noun is singular or plural. The idea of number, which indeed truly attaches only to the noun itself, is indicated but once. It seems hardly accurate, then, to say concerning Modern English that the verb always agrees with the subject in number or that the adjective always agrees with the noun it modifies. Certainly there is no such agreement as one finds in Latin, or in Greek, or in the older stages of the English language. The conventional rules concerning agreement in number are part of the Latin syntax that our makers of school grammars have tried to import into English. They apply to an inflected language like Latin, Greek, or Old English, but not to Modern English.

But, it may be objected, there are a few cases in which secondary words do show number in Modern English. There are the demonstrative pronouns "that" and "this" with plural forms "those" and "these"; there is the difference in the verb (indicative mood, third person, present tense) between "he speaks" and "they speak," or "he is" and "they are." These give the trouble and our objector would insist that the rules will in these cases serve as the guide to the correct forms. As applied to the verb, for instance, the rule would mean that wherever the form of the noun is singular there the verb (if

it is third person, indicative, present) must also show the form to indicate singular number.

As a matter of fact, however, there are many cases of actual usage where this agreement of form is not carried out. I can say, for example, "The family is here" or "The family *are* all here," depending upon whether I have more prominently in mind the family as a single unit or the individuals who make up the group. The word "family," however, is grammatically singular in form and in the older English the verb used with it would also have the form indicating singular number. The agreement in Latin, or in Greek, or in Old English is an agreement based primarily on form. In Modern English, that form of the verb is used which accords with the meaning in the subject. If the meaning is singular as in "five years" taken as one unit of time the forms of both the demonstrative and the verb will follow that meaning as, *"This* last *five years has* been a time of reconstruction." If the meaning is plural the forms of the verb will be plural as, "There are two thousand foreigners on the boat of whom *one half were* Italians." In other words, in Modern English in the very few cases where forms indicating number still remain in verbs and adjectives, there is a strong tendency toward an agreement based not on grammatical form but on the meaning.

In most situations the meaning and the form

singular meaning dominates the singular forms in the first part of the sentences but the plural idea in the situation comes to the surface and determines the forms in the latter part of the sentences.

"*Every* English *man* and *woman has* good reason to be proud of the work done by *their* forefathers in prose and poetry." (Stopford Brooke, *Primer of English Literature,* p. 5.)

"Our *club has* frequently caught him tripping, at which times *they* never spare him." (Addison, *Spectator,* No. 105.)

"*Each House* shall keep a journal of *its proceedings,* and from time to time publish the same, excepting such parts as may in *their* judgment require secrecy. . . ." (*Constitution of the United States,* Article I, Section 5, No. 3.)

If, then, we must decide a question of English grammar in which agreement in number is the issue, what shall we say? Usage cannot be the basis of the decision for the examples reveal considerable difference of usage. The conventional rules are perfectly clear, insisting that "the verb should agree in number with the subject," that "a pronoun should agree with its antecedent in number," and that "an adjective must agree in number with the noun it modifies." But these rules imply an inflectional system like Latin or Old English, a condition which does not exist in Modern English. The history of the English language shows an almost complete losing of inflections for number in secondary words and a developing tendency to use the very few number forms still remaining in accord with an agreement based on meaning rather than form. Where agreement in number is the issue I should insist that, although no one set of forms is the sole correct one because of the division of usage, it would be a reasonable and sound decision to choose the one that is in harmony with the tendencies of the development of our language as these can be seen from its history. This method is but yielding to those patterns which constitute the genius of the English language.

Another illustration may aid in clarifying further the application of this principle to guide decisions in cases of divided usage. What is the correct plural form of the word "formula"? Shall we insist that the plural form must continue to be "formulae" rather than "formulas"? Of all the ways by which the plural was expressed in Old English the so-called -s ending (belonging originally to but one class of nouns, the masculine a-stems) has become the pattern in Modern English. There still remain in the English language very few exceptions that have resisted the pull of this pattern. Very definitely the tendency of English has been toward this -s ending to express the plural of nouns. When the child says "three tooths" he does not do so because he has heard the form "tooths" and reproduces it. He has simply learned the pattern by which Modern English indicates plural number and he creates the form "tooths" in accord with that pattern. The few forms like "teeth" which have not yet gone over to the pattern must be learned by repetition. Wherever there is, then, a problem of divided usage in which the form of the plural ending of the noun is the issue, I should prefer the -s ending that is in accord with the tendency of the language. "Formulas" is such a form or even "phenomena" as a singular and "phenomenas" as a plural.[4]

If then we dismiss the conventional rules of our common school grammars as standards by which to measure the forms and constructions of our language we may give a practical answer to the question "What English is grammatically acceptable?" in the following three statements:

1. The only basis for correctness in grammar must be usage, for the schools the usage of those who are carrying on the affairs of English-speaking people.

2. Where this usage is practically unanimous there is no appeal, but where it is divided no one form or construction is the sole correct one.

3. In cases of divided usage a reasonable guiding principle of decision would be to choose that form or construction which is in accord with the tenden-

[4] Compare *opera* and *operas*.

cies or patterns of English as these can be seen from the history of the language.

If the point of view here set forth is sound it is obvious that we need a school grammar which differs from the type usually published. We need a grammar that describes the forms and syntax of present-day American English accurately; a grammar that records the facts of the actual usage of those who are carrying on the affairs of English-speaking people and does not falsify the account in accord with a make-believe standard of "school-mastered" speech; a grammar that explains these facts in the light of their history, not by means of an *a priori* reasoning; and finally, a grammar that attempts to set forth the patterns or tendencies that have shown themselves in the drift of the English language.

SELECTED REFERENCES

Academy Papers, Addresses on Language Problems by Members of the American Academy of Arts and Letters (Published by Charles Scribner's Sons, 1925).

BRADLEY, WILLIAM, *The Making of English,* Chapter II.

GRATTAN and GURREY, *Our Living Language,* Intro., Chapters I, II.

HALL, J. LESLIE, *English Usage.*

JESPERSON, OTTO, L*anguage: Its Nature, Development, and Origin,* Chapters VII, XVII, XVIII, XIX, XXI.

KRAPP, G. P., *Modern English, Its Growth and Present Use*, Chapters I, IV, VII, VIII.

KRAPP, G. P., *The English Language in America*, Vol. II, Chap. III.

LOUNSBURY, T. R., *The Standard of Usage in English*.

MATTHEWS, BRANDER, *Parts of Speech*, Chapter IX.

SAPIR, EDWARD, *Language*, Chapter VII.

STURTEVANT, E. H., *Linguistic Change*, Chapters VI, VII, VIII.

WYLD, H. C., *History of Modern Colloquial English*, Chapter I.

WYLD, H. C., *Elementary Lessons in English Grammar*.

Preliminary Report of the Grammar Subcommittee, Committee on Economy of Time for the National Council of Teachers of English, *English Journal*, Vol. VIII, 179-189. (March, 1919.)

The Teaching of English in England (Government Report, 1922), Chapter IX, Section I, pp. 278-294.

CHAPTER III

"Somwhat he lipsed, for his wantonesse,
  To make his English swete up-on his tonge;"

ALTHOUGH lisping in "wantonesse" may have gone out of fashion, the effort of Chaucer's Friar "to make his English swete up-on his tonge" still lives. Some find this sweetness in imitating a few sounds of the British pronunciation of southern England; some in struggling to conquer the vowel sounds of an older New England; some in reproducing the intonations peculiar to our southern "quality." Our schools, however, seem less concerned with cultivating a charming speech than with trying to develop "correct pronunciation." And just as the rules of the common school grammars have been looked upon as the infallible guide to correct constructions so our purists in pronunciation have usually found measures of a similar character which furnished the objects of their idolatry.

46

The most common of these idols to be worshipped as the infallible guide to correct pronunciation is the pronouncing dictionary and those books of lesser dignity, the little handbooks of "correct speech."[1] Of course the attitude upon which this practice rests is simply another manifestation and survival of the eighteenth century views of language. The dictionaries, like the grammars, have fulfilled the function of an "academy" in setting up standards by which to judge good speech from bad. Thus whenever a question arises concerning any pronunciation the first impulse of most of us is to ask, "What does the dictionary say?" It is practically always *the* dictionary that is called for, as if there were but one; we never specify a particular one. And despite the date of publication, the pronunciation recorded in any dictionary, elementary or unabridged, or in any speech manual which happens to be at hand, is accepted as the *correct* one. Fortunately for our faith we seldom consult more than one book for the same word and thus raise no questions concerning the disagreements of the various "authorities."

To be convinced that such disagreements exist one needs only to consult the lists given in the

[1] Typical handbooks are Vizetelly's *A Desk-Book of 25,000 Words Frequently Mispronounced*, Pfeif's *18,000 Words often Mispronounced*, and J. W. Abernethy's *Correct Pronunciation, a Manual of 2000 Common Words Frequently Mispronounced*.

unabridged editions of both Webster's *New International Dictionary* and the *Standard Dictionary*. In the latter the "Disputed Pronunciations" occupy pages 2763 to 2779 inclusive, a list of more than 2200 words. A similar list of something over 1600 words is given in the former dictionary, pages LX to LXXV. Both lists contain only those words in respect to which the important dictionaries record and prefer essentially different pronunciations. An interesting as well as an enlightening exercise for one who has never tried it is to record first his own pronunciation of some words like those in the following list, and then to note and compare the pronunciations given in at least four different dictionaries:[2] *Asiatic, adult, Christian, glacial, nausea, suggest, codify, isthmus, gaseous, apron.*

Of course it would be a perfectly reasonable attitude to insist that any pronunciation appearing in any dictionary is to be approved; that where dictionaries differ the variant sounds are equally acceptable. Too frequently in practice, however, the pronunciation recorded in the particular book consulted is not only accepted as *a* correct one but as *the* correct one and all others condemned as wrong. Thus to use a dictionary as a final authority of

[2] The four outstanding dictionaries of today seem to be *The New English Dictionary* (also frequently called the *Oxford English Dictionary*), *The Century Dictionary*, *Webster's New International Dictionary*, and *The Standard Dictionary*.

correct pronunciation and to condemn all variations from the one or two renderings there recorded is entirely contrary to the views of the editors of our recent dictionaries,[3] if their statements as given in the prefaces fairly represent their attitude toward the marking of pronunciation.

"The function of a pronouncing dictionary is to record as far as possible the pronunciations prevailing in the best present usage, rather than to attempt to dictate what that usage should be. In so far as a dictionary may be known and acknowledged as a faithful recorder and interpreter of such usage, so far and no farther may it be appealed to as an authority. . . .

"In the case of diverse usages of extensive prevalence, the dictionary must recognize each of them, preferring that pronunciation which is used by the majority of the well-educated; . . .

"Even when the actual usage to be adopted as a standard is determined upon, only approximation to exactness can be attained in its indication. The sounds which must be indicated by the same symbol are often subject to a considerable variation as spoken, not only by members of different communities, but also, frequently by members of the same community. . . .

"There exist . . . especially in some of the vowel

[3] The editors of the older dictionaries, those of the latter part of the eighteenth century and the early nineteenth century, did attempt to legislate on the matter of pronunciations. See for example the quotations from the dictionaries given in Chapter I.

sounds, actual variations in pronunciation (all equally good, or allowable) that are so wide as to require special mention. Such, for example, are the sounds of *o* in *glory*, and the *a* in *vary*. The vowel sounds indicated in marking pronunciations are rarely invariable; what is marked in any case is the average or typical sound, around which the one actually spoken may vary according to conditions." [4]

"Correctness in pronunciation, like correctness in diction, depends upon the consensus of usage among educated people. There are many words in the language regarding the correct pronunciation of which expert orthoepists and scholars as well as dictionaries do not agree. The correctness of English pronunciation should obviously be determined by the best and widest usage among the English speaking people." [5]

"Still greater than the variation in the orthography, even the accepted orthography, of English words, is the variation in the pronunciation. . . . No attempt is made to record all the varieties of popular, or even of educated, utterance, or to report the determinations made by different recognized authorities. It has been necessary, rather, to make a selection of words to which alternative pronunciations should be accorded, and to give preference among these according to the circumstances of each particular case, in view of the general analogies and tendencies of English utterance." [6]

[4] *Webster's New International Dictionary*, pp. XXXVIII, XXXIX.
[5] *The Standard Dictionary*, p. XII.
[6] *The Century Dictionary*, p. XIII.

"From the composite character of the English Vocabulary, the pronunciation, also, of many words is in a very unsettled state. This is the fact not merely with words from other modern languages, the pronunciation of which depends largely upon the linguistic knowledge and taste of the person who uses them, but also with derivatives from Latin or Greek, for which there exist two or more analogies. . . . The conflict of analogies, or the absence of any analogy, appears still more in purely scientific words, in which there may be said to be no general standard of pronunciation. The Editor was once present at a meeting of a learned society, where, in the course of discussion, he heard the word *gaseous* systematically pronounced in six different ways by as many eminent physicists." [7]

Two more considerations must be kept in mind in our attempt to judge the dictionaries as measures of correct pronunciation. It is to be noted, first, that although all these editors insist that correctness of pronunciation must rest fundamentally upon usage there has never been a comprehensive and scientific survey of English pronunciation and thus the records offered in any book are necessarily limited to the observations of the particular staff who worked on it. Our trust in the validity of the markings must depend solely upon our faith in the *opinions* of those individuals who edited the dictionary. More than that, all agree that usage in the matter

[7] *The New English Dictionary,* p. XXIV.

of pronunciation is continually changing. As a record of usage, therefore, any dictionary, by the time the material has been collected and printed, and the books offered for sale, is already behind the times. In some respects, at least, usage will have changed and the printed record be inaccurate.

Second, most of us need to be reminded that all our dictionaries (with the exception of the great *Oxford English Dictionary*) have been the product of private business enterprises. Quite frankly the purposes of these firms have been neither philanthropic nor scientific; they have invested capital in the making of books that would sell and return a profit. In line with good business policy they have sought the best editors and staff they could secure for the salaries they could afford to pay but have seldom attracted to the actual work of dictionary making the very best scholars in the field of English language. The particular materials to be included in the dictionaries have been dictated primarily by the practical considerations of selling values. As a policy, no such dictionaries, even for the sake of scientific truth and language accuracy, could afford to oppose the prejudices and the common beliefs of the school public which buys the dictionaries. That public has demanded an authoritative standard of pronunciation and the dic-

tionaries have in practice provided it [8] despite the
careful statements of some editors to the contrary.
Our blind faith in *the dictionary* as the authoritative
measure of right and wrong in pronunciation has
called forth from our scholars in the English language
such statements as the following from the late
Professor T. R. Lounsbury of Yale University:

"It seems never to have occurred to any of the
compilers of dictionaries, and to but few of those who
consult them, that the simple solution of the whole
difficulty is that in the matter of pronunciation there
is no standard of authority at all. Nor, as things
now are, can there be. Pronunciation must and
will vary widely among persons of equal intelligence
and cultivation. A dictionary which sets out to
establish on a solid base an authoritative standard
is bound to take into account the practice of the
whole body of educated men the world over who
are entitled to consideration. How is that to be
ascertained? The mere statement of the fact shows
its physical impossibility. It is a task beyond the
power of any one person or any number of persons
to accomplish.

"Even this is not the worst. If everybody worth
consulting could be consulted, we should still be left
in precisely the same state of uncertainty in which
we were before. . . . Still this belief in the existence of a standard authority is one that will die hard

[8] G. & C. Merriam Company advertize *Webster's New International Dictionary* as "The 'Supreme Authority'."

even with the educated class. With the semi-educated class it will never die at all." [9]

A second idol reverenced by many as a sound guide to correct pronunciation is the spelling. Mr. Vizetelly says, for example,

"Unfortunately, we have with us a large class of persons who speak without thinking how our words are spelled, and who, therefore, squeeze all the juice out of our speech by refusing to enunciate carefully all the niceties of sound that the words contain." [10]

It seems also to be a regard for the spelling which lies at the basis of such rules as the following:

"Pronounce clearly and distinctly the first syllables of words beginning with *be* or *de:*

de cide	*not*	di *or* duhcide
de note	*not*	di *or* dunote
de test	*not*	di *or* duhtest
be lieve	*not*	bi *or* buhlieve."

"Pronounce carefully the final syllables in the following words:

fountain	*not*	fountun
mountain	*not*	mountun
certain	*not*	certun
Boston	*not*	Bostun

---

[9] T. R. Lounsbury, *The Standard of Pronunciation in English*, pp. 213–216.

[10] F. H. Vizetelly, *A Desk-Book of 25,000 Words Frequently Mispronounced*, p. VIII.

pupil	*not*	pupul
angel	*not*	angul
hovel	*not*	hovul." [11]

From this point of view it is insisted that the *spelling* demands four syllables in the pronunciation of *usually* and three in *every;* that there must be no "p" [12] in *warmth,* or in *something,* or in *comfort;* that

---

[11] Annie E. Polk, *Better Speech,* p. 13.

[12] In every written discussion of pronunciation one must use some system of symbols to indicate sounds. In this book the following simplified form of phonetic notation will be used and in each instance, in order to distinguish pronunciations from spellings, will be enclosed in brackets. It is in the main the alphabet of the International Phonetic Association and very generally used.

Symbol					*Key Word*
a	the vowel		sound in		pod
æ	" "		"	"	pal
ɛ	" "		"	"	pear
e	" "		"	"	pale
ę	" "		"	"	pelt
i	" "		"	"	peal
ı̣	" "		"	"	pill
o	" "		"	"	pole
ɔ	" "		"	"	Paul
u	" "		"	"	pool
ų	" "		"	"	pull
ʌ	" "		"	"	pulp
ə	" 2nd vowel		"	"	China
ɚ	" "		"	"	pearl
ai	" diphthong		"	"	pile
au	" "		"	"	pouch
ı̣u	" "		"	"	puny
ɔi	" "		"	"	point

Arctic has a *c* in the first syllable and must therefore be pronounced [arktịk]; that *recognize* is spelled with a *g* and is therefore correctly pronounced [rękagnaiz]; that in the words *hundred* and *children* the *r* precedes the *e* in the final syllable and therefore these words must be pronounced [hʌndrẹd] and [tʃịldrẹn] not [hʌndərd] and [tʃịldərn]; and finally that the vowels in the unstressed syllables of words, to be pronounced correctly, must be given the sounds of the letters with which they are spelled and not reduced to the obscure and colorless [ə] sound.

b	the initial	consonant	sound	in	bin
d	"	"	"	"	" din
f	"	"	"	"	" ffne
g	"	"	"	"	" gate
h	"	"	"	"	" hate
j	"	"	"	"	" yell
k	"	"	"	"	" Kate
l	"	"	"	"	" lake
m	"	final	"	"	" ɲum
n	"	"	"	"	" run
ŋ	"	"	"	"	" rung
p	"	initial	"	"	" pin
r	"	"	"	"	" rake
s	"	final	"	"	" race
ʃ	"	first	"	"	" assure
ʒ	"	"	"	"	" azure
t	"	initial	"	"	" tin
θ	"	"	"	"	" thin
ð	"	"	"	"	" then
v	"	"	"	"	" vine
w	"	"	"	"	" weal
hw	"	"	"	"	" wheel
z	"	final	"	"	" raise

This view underlies the arguments offered in many discussions of correct pronunciation although it is not often expressly stated as a general principle. In attempting to test its validity three considerations demand attention.

First, the editors of at least three of our most important dictionaries have, in the prefaces to those works, made vigorous statements condemning the approach to modern English pronunciation through the spelling.

"The pronunciation is the actual living form or forms of a word, that is, *the word itself*, of which the current spelling is only a symbolization—generally, indeed, only the traditionally-preserved symbolization of an earlier form, sometimes imperfect to begin with, still oftener corrupted in its passage to our time. . . .

"In modern English speech, vowels are regularly obscured in syllables that have neither primary nor secondary stress, especially in those that follow the main stress; they then approach, or fall into, the sound of the mid-mixed vowel or [ə]."[13]

"One of the most peculiar characteristics of English pronunciation is the way in which it slights the vowels of most unaccented syllables, not merely lightening them in point of quantity and stress, but changing their quality of sound. To write (as systems of re-spelling for pronunciation, and even systems of phonetic spelling generally do) the

[13] *The New English Dictionary*, Preface, p. XXIV.

vowels of unaccented syllables as if they were accented, is a distortion, and to pronounce them as so written would be a caricature of English speech."[14]

"The spoken form of language is always more changeable than the written form, and changes in pronunciation are only slowly reflected in the spelling. Moreover since the invention of printing, English spelling has tended to become more and more conventional and fixed, while changes in pronunciation have continued. One has only to call to mind such common words as *busy, bosom, colonel, women, bough, enough, tough, night*, to realize how unphonetic their spelling is with reference to their present pronunciation. Again the written forms of some words, as *mountain, fountain, evil, devil, often, soften, Christmas, chestnut, handsome, handkerchief*, more nearly phonetic, mislead many persons, who feel that they should speak as they write, into pronunciations that depart from the best usage by making *-tain* rime with *rain*, *-il* rime with *hill*, by sounding the *t* in *often, Christmas*, etc."[15]

Second, the general principle of "pronouncing all the letters of our words as they are now spelled" is not only incapable of any wide application because of the acknowledged unphonetic character of the spelling of many words but it is also incapable of consistent application even in any narrow group of words. Not even the strongest advocate of spelling as the guide to pronunciation would dare sound the

[14] *The Century Dictionary*, Preface, p. xiv, xv.
[15] *Webster's New International Dictionary*, Preface, p. xxxviii.

following words as they are spelled: *deign, sovereign, foreign, doubt, debt, island, aisle, know, knight, knee, knave, mortgage, any, many, English, two, whole, fatigue, tongue, ghost, does, calm, limb, lamb, sepulchre, choir, answer, sword, write.* Nor can one pronounce in any single way the same groups of letters. What, for instance should be the single sound given to the combination *ing* in the following words: *singer, finger, ginger?* What sound for the *eo* spelling in *Leopold, leopard, pigeon* and *people?* If *hoof, roof, root,* because of the *oo* spelling, must be pronounced as [huf], [ruf], [rut], and never [hu̯f], [ru̯f], [ru̯t], should we consistently demand the same pronunciation of the following words which historically had the same vowel sound and retain a similar spelling, *book, good, stood, hood, hook?* I did find one teacher, and that in a large city school system, who with the courage of strong conviction was bound to be consistent. She insisted that the word *laughter* since it was spelled like *daughter* and *slaughter* must be pronounced in similar fashion, thus, [lɔtər], and was drilling her pupils to pronounce it that way.

Even in the matter of following in pronunciation the order of the letters as they stand in the spelling one can hardly be consistent. He may say [hʌndrɛd] and [tʃɪldrɛn]; he may even school himself to say [eprən] rather than [epərn] for the word *apron.* He will hardly, however, say [airən] for the word *iron* rather than [aiərn]. If he does he invents a pronunciation, one not recorded in any of our dictionaries nor heard in the usage of people.

As a third consideration respecting the validity of spelling as a guide to correct pronunciation one must view a few of the important facts in the history of English spelling.[16] "How came we to spell as we do, and how is it that the written symbol so frequently gives a totally false impression of the true sound of the spoken word?" Although the writing of French shows probably a greater "divergence between sound and symbol," "English shows the maximum of irregularity and arbitrariness."[17] During the Old English period (*i.e.*, before 1100 A. D.) and even during a large part of the Middle English period (1100–1500) the spelling of English was fairly phonetic and changed with the changing pronunciation. Consistency of spelling was not then a virtue. Chaucer, for instance, spells the word *high* in three different ways within a space of fifty lines, thus:

[16] The history of English spelling is treated at some length by W. W. Skeat in *Principles of English Etymology*, First Series, Chapter XVI (pp. 294–333), and is touched upon by A. J. Ellis in *Early English Pronunciation*, Chapter VI (pp. 565–632), and by Henry Sweet in *A History of English Sounds*, pp. 59–73.

[17] Encyclopædia Britannica, article *Phonetics*, 11th edition, Vol. 21, p. 459.

"and hye on horse he sat"   A-271[18]
"and ful of hy sentence"   A-301
"and for his heigh renoun"   A-316

Differences in spelling usually furnished some evidence of differences in sound. Even at this time, however, the spelling not only lagged behind changes in pronunciation, but it had been subjected to such treatment as further to spoil its phonetic accuracy. The practice of doubling vowel letters to indicate vowel length (hōf—hoof, hrōf—roof, bōk—book, cwēn—queen) was only partly carried out as was also that other practice of doubling the consonant after a short vowel (biter—bitter, soper—supper, somer—summer). Many long vowels still remained single in spelling and many short vowels were still followed by single consonants (meddle, medal; mettle, metal; copper, proper). The respelling of the language by Anglo-French scribes in the thirteenth and fourteenth centuries accounts for many changes from the particular letters in use during the Old English period. Thus, for example, *cw* was replaced by *qu*, þ and ð were replaced by *th*, and *c* was used at times to represent the sound [s].

The two most important facts in the development of English spelling for our view here, however, are matters of the fifteenth and sixteenth centuries.

---

[18] This instance should probably not be included, for *hye* is here an adverb, not an adjective as it is in the other instances.

First, the introduction of printing and the increase of books worked to crystallize or conventionalize the spelling and prevent it from further adapting itself to the pronunciation. From the printers' point of view the ideal spelling is one that is absolutely uniform and unchangeable. It has been this influence that has led to the setting up of "correct" spelling and adherence to this *uniformity* as a skill to be cultivated.

At the time that the influence of the printers was making for a hard and fast system of spelling, the so-called "etymological" idea was introduced. The sixteenth-century pedants, who were enthusiastic for the classics, attempted to find traces of Latin in English words. Some, indeed, insisted that all the English language came from Latin. In order then to render this connection between English and Latin words more evident to the eye they changed the spellings of many words. Of course this kind of etymologizing could be applied to but a part of the language. It was the learned words rather than the very common words which were thus treated to "etymological" spelling. Unfortunately the scholarship of these pedants was unequal even to the task of dealing with the learned words of the vocabulary, and they introduced many errors. Thus an *s* was inserted in the word *island* to show a connection with the Latin word *insula*, although *island* (spelled by Chaucer *iland*) is not in any way related to *insula* but is in fact a good old Anglo-Saxon word, *ig-land*, meaning *water-land*. Many of these errors still exist and account for some of the worst of our present spellings; witness, for instance, the *g* in *sovereign* and in *foreign*.

English spelling since the sixteenth century has been dominated by two principles. The phonetic principle has applied to popular words and the so-called "etymological" principle has applied to the more learned words. But neither principle has been carried out consistently even in its own province. More than that, pronunciation changes since the sixteenth century have been very great while spelling changes have been comparatively few. We have thus today a petrified system of spelling which very imperfectly represented the pronunciation of English during the time of Shakespeare but is now used to represent a twentieth century pronunciation. With such a situation, despite the fact that there is enough phonetic connection between the written symbols and the word sounds to enable us to guess approximately the pronunciation of many words we cannot ever be sure as to any particular word and we cannot by any means accept the view of Dr. Johnson "to consider those as the most elegant speakers who deviate least from the written words." [19]

[19] Samuel Johnson, Preface to *Dictionary*, 1755.

In addition to dependence upon the spelling as the basis for determining the proper sounds of words and the reverence for the pronouncing dictionaries as the authority, there is a third idol very generally worshipped as a guide to *correct* pronunciation. It is the principle that borrowed words must continue their sounds from the language from which they come. From this point of view it is asserted that the only correct pronunciation for a borrowed French word is the sound which that word has in French; that the "analogies" of the Latin language should determine the pronunciation of Latin words in English. Thus in application of this view, it is demanded that *inquiry* should be pronounced [ɪnkwai′rɪ] never [ɪ′nkwɪrɪ]; that *acclimate* must be [æklai′mɪt] never [æ′klɪmet]; that *arbutus* must be stressed on the first syllable and *abdomen* on the second. By similar reasoning it is insisted that *prestige* must be pronounced [prɛsti′ʒ] never [prɛ′stɪdʒ], and *garage* always [gəra′ʒ] never [gəra′dʒ] and certainly not [gæ′rɪdʒ].

As a matter of fact it is the borrowed words in our language which cause many of the problems of pronunciation. English has an immense number of these foreign words from many sources. Nearly half of our vocabulary is made up of words from the Latin language, if we include as Latin element both direct borrowings from Latin itself and also those

words that have come through French. Some of
these borrowed words remain learned words, re-
stricted in their use to those people who are likely
to have some familiarity with the language from
which they come. These words cling to their foreign
sounds and accent even after centuries of use.
Thus *caprice*, a seventeenth-century borrowing,
shows in usage no signs of shifting from its present
pronunciation, [kəpri′s]. It is not a word used by
the ordinary man of the street. On the other hand,
words which become popular and are used by many
who are unfamiliar with the sounds of the foreign
language tend to a pronunciation adjusted to
English sounds and English stress. Thus the word
garage, although of comparatively recent importa-
tion, is used by people of all stations in life for almost
every family has one. The Englishing of the
pronunciation of this word has come rather quickly.
In many communities it has become [gæ′rɪdʒ];
certainly [gəra′dʒ] is more general than [gəra′ʒ].

As a principle to guide pronunciation the attempt
to continue the foreign sound of a borrowed word
is impossible of consistent application.[20] Even

[20] It is really impossible for most of us to jump suddenly into
the speech pattern of a foreign language in the midst of an
English sentence. Our rendering of the pronunciation of a
foreign word is, therefore, only approximately correct, rarely
accurate. See, for instance, the comment of Jespersen in *How
to Teach a Foreign Language* (p. 92).

"Let me remark in passing that I have always given my

those who are most careful to observe the foreign sounds of the comparatively few words to which their attention happens to be directed would not, in accord with that principle, insist upon stressing the following words on the next to the last syllable, *audi'tor*, *ora'tor*, *sena'tor*, *victo'ry*. If this principle is sufficient ground for condemning the pronunciation [gæ'rɪdʒ] as incorrect, then to pronounce *courage* and *carriage* as most of us do is equally incorrect. Even in the matter of foreign proper names the principle of preserving the foreign pronunciations cannot be maintained in the cases of names that become very generally used. The word *Paris* is a case in point, or the name *Beatrice*.

In passing, we need but call attention to the fact that most of those who cling to the belief that a word borrowed from another language is correctly pronounced only when it maintains the foreign sounds apply the principle only to words from those languages with which they happen to be familiar. Words from Arabic or Hebrew or the American Indian languages are Englished with no apologies. In the pronunciation of the many foreign words in our language, therefore, we cannot accept this principle as the standard of acceptable pronunciation.

pupils French names [in classes in French] immediately in one of the first lessons; . . . the teacher has the advantage of being able to use their names in the middle of a French sentence without marring the run of the language.''

If, then, we must repudiate all three of the measures of correct pronunciation so commonly used what can we offer as the standards of acceptable English speech? First of all, the actual sound of the word as it is heard in the present usage of English speakers, not the spelling, not the etymology, must be the basis of all the "correctness" there can be in pronunciation. The *practical* standard of pronunciation must thus be the speech of those we actually *hear*. With the development in means of communication, increasing travel and moving from place to place, and especially the rapidly spreading use of the radio, these personal contacts are likely to have a much wider range than formerly and, as a result, there ought to be an increasing number of people with speech characteristics of approximate similarity. Certainly those who carry on the affairs of English-speaking people are now more frequently and more widely heard by voice than could have been possible in preceding times. I should insist, then, that the pronunciations common in the usage of those in positions of influence and respect must furnish the starting point for determining what is acceptable English in respect to pronunciation.

When one examines this usage, even superficially, he discovers very soon that the same word is frequently pronounced differently *by the same person* when used in differing circumstances. We must conclude, then, that there is no *one* pronunciation of a word that is the true pronunciation for that word under all circumstances. The amount of stress given the word in a sentence and the character of the surrounding sounds must organically affect the pronunciation. The word *him,* for instance, stressed in such a sentence as "Give it to hím, not to Máry," has a very distinct initial [h]. But in the following sentence, with a heavy stress on the words *to* and *from,* "Give it tó him—don't take it fróm him," the initial aspirate disappears and the word becomes [ɪm]. Again, no one actually speaking *English* would give the same sounds to both the conjunction *that* and the demonstrative *that* in such a combination as "in order *that that* nation might endure." This difference between the sounds of words when pronounced alone or under stress and when sounded in an unemphasized part of a sentence the dictionaries generally recognize. Such recognition, however, is usually expressed only in the preface and most of us miss it.

"The difference between the pronunciation of a word when taken alone and as it occurs in a sentence should also be kept carefully in mind; thus *and* considered alone is *and,* but in such a combination as *bread and butter* it is usually weakened to *'nd,* or even to *'n; a* in the phrase *for a day* becomes *a* (sof' *a*), etc." [21]

[21] *Webster's New International Dictionary,* Preface, p. xxxviii.

Again, even a superficial examination of the pronunciation of those speakers of English in positions of respect and influence reveals also the fact that there are many differences in these pronunciations from speaker to speaker. The lists of the so-called "disputed pronunciations" in our dictionaries (see above page 48) offer some evidence for this assertion. As in the case of grammar, the problems arise out of these differences of usage. It is because many people who rightfully claim our respect pronounce the word *suggest* [sədʒɛst] and many others meriting equal respect insist on the pronunciation [səgdʒɛst] that we raise the question as to which is the *correct* sound. When these differences amount to more than mere individual peculiarities and become really significant divisions of usage, one can maintain the following point of view:

(1) Where this general spoken usage differs in respect to the sound of any word, no *one* pronunciation is the *sole* correct one. The several pronunciations in actual usage are thereby acceptable.[22]

---

[22] The very definite use of ambiguous symbols in the dictionaries would substantiate this view. In the Preface of the *New English Dictionary* (p. XXIV) we have the following, "The vowel in pass, command, variously identified by different speakers with *a* in man, and *a* in father, is symbolized by the avowedly ambiguous ɑ. Similarly, the doubtful length of the *o* in off, soft, lost (by some made *short* as in got, by some long as in Corfe, by others medial) is indicated by ǫ." In this connection I must again call attention to the fact that I am in these chapters dis-

(2) In such cases of divided usage, however, a reasonable choice may be made in accord with the following considerations:

(a) In the matter of borrowed words, for that pronunciation which is in harmony with English sounds and English accent.

(b) For that pronunciation which is in harmony with the tendencies of English speech in the matters of unstressed vowels, and organically phonetic assimilations of consonants.

Concerning the unstressed vowels the quotations from *The New English Dictionary* and *The Century Dictionary*, given above on pages 57 and 58, indicate the practice in English.

Phonetic assimilation in the case of consonants is illustrated in part by the following quotation from *The Century Dictionary*.

"On the side of consonant utterance, there is a very large class of cases where it can be made a question whether a pure *t* or *d* or *s* or *z* is pronounced with an *i*- or *y*-sound after it before another vowel or whether the consonant is fused together with the *i* or *y* into the sounds *ch*, *j*, *sh*, *zh* respectively—for example, whether we say *natūre* or *nachur*, *gradūal* or *grajöal*, *sūre* or *shör*, *vizūal* or *vizhöal*. There are many such words in which accepted usage has fully ranged itself on the side of the fused pronunciation: for

cussing standards of *acceptable* English, not the problem of *beautiful* or *artistic* language.

example, *vizhon*, not *vizion*, for vision; *azhur*, not *ızūre* for azure; but with regard to the great majority usage is less decided, or else the one pronunciation is given in ordinary easy utterance and the other when speaking with deliberation or labored plainness, or else the fused pronunciation is used without the fact being acknowledged." [23]

Other examples of such assimilations are the following pronunciations: *chestnut* as [tʃɛsnət], *friends* as [frɛnz], *something* as [sʌmpθɪŋ], *length* as [lɛŋkθ], *ink* as [ɪŋk], *handkerchief* as [hæŋkərtʃif], *pumpkin* as [pʌŋkɪn].

(c) For that pronunciation which maintains a careful discrimination of those sounds that the English speech pattern uses to distinguish many meanings. Two quotations may aid to clarify this point although it is by no means simple.

"The latitude of correctness is very far from being the same in different languages. Some sounds in each language move within narrow boundaries, while others have a much larger field assigned to them; each language is punctilious in some, but not in all points. Deviations which in one language would be considered trifling, in another would be intolerable perversions." [24]

The voiced or voiceless character of the consonants

[23] *The Century Dictionary*, Preface, p. XIV.
[24] Otto Jespersen, *Language*, p. 283.

and the quality of the vowel sounds in stressed syllables are examples of such important points in the English speech pattern. Thus, for instance we distinguish many words simply by a differentiation of a single vowel sound: heat [hit], hit [hɪt], hate [het], hat [hæt], hut [hʌt], hot [hat], hoot [hut], height [hait]. Examples of differentiation by means of voicing only are the following: pin–bin, tin–din, cold–gold, fine–vine.

The second quotation touches my point from another angle:

"I found that it was difficult or impossible to teach an Indian to make phonetic distinctions that did not correspond to 'points in the pattern of his language,' however these differences might strike our objective ear, but that subtle, barely audible, phonetic differences, if only they hit the 'points in the pattern,' were easily and voluntarily expressed in writing. In watching my Nootka interpreter write his language, I often had the curious feeling that he was transcribing an ideal flow of phonetic elements which he heard inadequately from a purely objective standpoint, as the intention of the actual rumble of speech." [25]

If the view of English pronunciation given in this chapter has any validity it must be evident that in dealing with matters of pronunciation, especially in attempting to determine what is acceptable English

[25] Edward Sapir, *Language*, p. 58 (footnote).

speech, it is well to cultivate the virtue of tolerance. There is comparatively little difficulty in settling upon some one pronunciation for any word that must be acknowledged acceptable. Justly to render a negative judgment, however, to condemn any pronunciation that one hears generally used, demands much greater caution as well as knowledge. The suggestions here given as considerations to guide one's choice in matters of divided usage are to be taken as standards of acceptable pronunciation only from the positive point of view. It must not be assumed that all other pronunciations are necessarily unacceptable.

SELECTED REFERENCES

BLOOMFIELD, LEONARD, *The Study of Language*, Chapter II.

DEWITT, M. E., *Euphon English in America.*

JESPERSEN, OTTO, *Modern English Grammar*, Vol. I, especially Chapters XIV, XV, XVI.

JESPERSEN, OTTO, *Language, Its Nature, Development and Origin*, Chapters V, IX, XIV, XV.

KENYON, J. S., *American Pronunciation.*

KRAPP, G. P., *English Language in America*, Vol. II, Chapter I.

KRAPP, G. P., *Modern English, Its Growth and Present Use*, Chapter V.

KRAPP, G. P., *The Pronunciation of Standard English in America.*

74 THE TEACHING OF ENGLISH

LOUNSBURY, THOMAS R., *The Standard of Pronunciation in English.*

LOUNSBURY, THOMAS R., *English Spelling and Spelling Reform.*

MATTHEWS, BRANDER, *Parts of Speech,* Chapters XII, XIII.

SAPIR, EDWARD, *Language,* Chapter III.

SAPIR, EDWARD, *Sound Patterns in Language,* in *Langauge,* Vol. I, pp. 37-51 (June, 1925).

SCOTT, F. N., *The Standard of American Speech.*

SKEAT, W. W., *Principles of English Etymology,* First Series, Chapter XVI.

WHITMAN, WALT, *The American Primer.*

WYLD, H. C., *The Historical Study of the Mother Tongue,* Chapters II, III, IV, XIV.

CHAPTER IV

Standards of Acceptable English: Vocabulary

Words have always been associated with magic. The belief in the power of spoken charms and incantations is fundamentally a belief in the magic power of words. To control this power one needed only to know the right names or words, and to use them in the proper combinations.

"Unable to discriminate clearly between words and things, the savage commonly fancies that the link between a name and the person or thing denominated by it is not a mere arbitrary and ideal association, but a real and substantial bond which unites the two in such a way that magic may be wrought on a man just as easily through his name as through his hair, his nails, or any other material part of his person. In fact, primitive man regards his name as a vital portion of himself and takes care of it accordingly. . . . The Tolampoos of central Celebes believe that if you write a man's name down you can carry off his soul along with it. On that account the headman of a village appeared uneasy when Mr. A. C. Ktuijt wrote down his name. He entreated the missionary to erase it, and was only reassured on being told that it was not his real name but merely his second name that had been put on paper. Again, when the same missionary took down the names of villages from the lips of a woman, she asked him anxiously if he would not thereby take away the soul of the villages and so cause the inhabitants to fall sick." [1]

"In the great primeval forest the Toradja feels ill at ease, for well he knows the choleric temper of the spirits who inhabit the giant trees of the wood, and that were he to excite their wrath they would assuredly pay him out in one way or other, it might be by carrying off his soul and so making him ill, it might be by crushing him under a falling tree. These touchy beings particularly dislike to hear certain words pronounced, and accordingly on his way through the forest the Toradja takes care to avoid the offensive terms and to substitute others for them. Thus he will not call a dog a dog, but refers to it as 'the hairy one'; a buffalo is spoken of as 'thick hide'; a cooking pot becomes 'that which is set down'; . . . goats and pigs are 'the folk under the house'; a horse is 'long nose'; and deer are 'denizens of the fell.' If he is rash or careless enough to utter a forbidden word in the forest, a short-tempered tree-spirit will fetch him such a bang on the head that the blood will spout from his nose and mouth. Again, when the weather is fine and the Toradja wishes it to continue so, he is careful not to utter the word 'rain,' for if he did so the rain

[1] J. G. Frazer, *Taboo and the Perils of the Soul,* pp. 318, 319.

would fancy he was called for and would obligingly present himself. Indeed, in the district of Pakambia, which is frequently visited by heavy storms, the word 'rain' may not be mentioned throughout the year lest it should provoke a tempest; the unmentionable thing is there delicately allured to as 'tree-blossoms.' " [2]

Although today we immediately recognize all this as part of the superstitions of undeveloped peoples, still there is much in our present popular view of *words* which perpetuates in principle the attitude of the past. To illustrate and discuss the general effect upon the English vocabulary of this attitude would carry us too far afield, although the subject is filled with interest. In passing to the particular aspects of this attitude that immediately concern us we can, however, call attention to at least two examples of the general effect of taboo among us. There is a feeling against speaking of death directly. We shun the words *die, dead, death,* when referring to persons, and use instead such phrases as *to pass away, to pass on, breathe his last, fall asleep, depart, to be no more, the deceased, the late Mr. —* There is also a feeling against the common use of the divine name. Especially disapproved is the use of the name, God, or Jesus, in exclamations. To escape this disapproval, instead of the actual for-

[2] J. G. Fraser, op. cit., pp. 412, 413.

bidden names, we use a curious assortment of substitutes in which some elements of the names are preserved but joined with other sounds. Thus for the word, *God,* we find *gosh, gol, golly, gorry, gad, Godfrey, goodness, goodness gracious.* As a substitute for the word, *Jesus,* we find *gee, geewhiz, geewhillikins, Jerusalem, jiminy, jiminy crickets* (the second word as a substitute for Christ), *cheese and crackers, Jehosaphat.*

The particular aspect of the primitive man's attitude toward words that concerns us here is the common feeling for an identity of the word with the thing it names. It is this feeling which underlies the belief that there is a *real* or *true meaning* for words which may or may not coincide with the content given them in usage. Ruskin thus argues concerning the word *wife:*

"The great value of the Saxon words is that they mean something. 'Wife' means weaver. You must be either house-wives or house-moths, remember that. In the deep sense, you must either weave men's fortunes and embroider them, or feed upon them and bring them to decay."

Carlyle uses similar reasoning in speaking of *kings.* He says:

"He is called *Rex,* Regulator, *Roi:* our own name is still better; King, *Könning,* which means *Can-*

ning, Able-man. . . . I say, Find me the true *Könning,* King or Able-man, and he *has* a divine right
over me."

This belief in a real or true meaning for words
aside from usage parallels the beliefs concerning
correct pronunciation and correct grammar discussed in the preceding chapters. Here, as in those
cases, there is frequently set up a *true* or *correct*
meaning for a word and then all uses of that word
which do not coincide with the particular meaning
are condemned as wrong. One has only to turn to
the manuals of correct English to find an abundance
of interesting examples.

It is insisted, for instance, that the word *metropolis* means *mother-city* and is properly used only in
an ecclesiastical sense. It is correctly applied, therefore, only to the chief *cathedral* city. Thus "Canter-
bury is the *metropolis* of England, but London is
not." It is held a gross misuse of the word to speak
of Chicago as a *metropolis.*

The true meaning of the word *insect,* it is asserted,
is *cut-in.* It is correctly applied, therefore, only to
those kinds of bugs which, like the wasp, have the
head joined to the abdomen by a very slender connection. The true *insect* seems thus to be notched
or nearly cut in two.

"*Aggravate* is misused by many persons ignorantly, and, in consequence, by many others thoughtlessly, in the sense of provoke, irritate, anger. Thus: He aggravates me by his impudence—meaning he angers me: Her martyr-like airs were very aggravating—the right word being irritating. . . . An insult may be aggravated by being offered to a man who is courteous and kindly, as it may be palliated by being offered to a brute and a bully. But it is no more proper to say in the one case that the person is aggravated, than in the other to say that he is palliated." [3]

We are told that *awful* means *awe-inspiring* and must not be used in any other sense; that *nice* means *minutely discriminating* and must never be used in the sense of *general approval;* that *balance* is "the difference between two sides of an account—the amount which is necessary to make one equal to the other"; to use it in the sense of "rest, remainder, residue, remnant, is an abomination."

In discussing the confusion of the words *people* and *persons* one writer says, "for twenty-five years or more I have kept my eye on this little word *people* and I have yet to find a single American or English author who does not misuse it." [4]

Not only are particular meanings of words con-

[3] Richard Grant White, *Words and Their Uses*, p. 88. See also H. W. Fowler, *Modern English Usage*, p. 13.

[4] Quoted by Brander Matthews, *Parts of Speech*, p. 226.

demned because they are considered to be incompatible with the true or correct meanings of these words, but also many widely used words are condemned because they seem illogically formed.

"Ice-water, Ice-cream.—By mere carelessness in enunciation these compound words have come to be used for *iced-water* and *iced-cream*—most incorrectly and with real confusion of language, if not of thought. For what is called ice-water is not made from ice, but is simply water iced, that is, made cold by ice; and ice-water might be warm, as snow-water often is. Ice-cream is unknown." [5]

"Donate.—I need hardly say, that this word is utterly abominable—one that any lover of simple honest English cannot hear with patience and without offence. It has been formed by some presuming and ignorant person from *donation*, and is much such a word as *vocate* would be from *vocation, orate* from *oration,* or *gradate* from *gradation;* and this when we have *give, present, grant, confer, endow, bequeath, devise,* with which to express the act of transferring possession in all its possible varieties." [6]

"Stand-point, whatever the channel of its coming into use, is of the sort to which the vulgar words *wash-tub, shoe-horn, brew-house, cook-stove,* and *go-cart* belong, the first four of which are merely slovenly and uncouth abbreviations of *washing-tub, shoeing-horn, brewing-house,* and *cooking-stove,* the

[5] R. G. White, op. cit., 127, 128.
[6] R. G. White, op. cit., pp. 205, 206.

last a nursery word, a counterpart to which would
be *rock-horse,* instead of *rocking-horse.* Compounds
of this kind are properly formed by the union of a
substantive or participle, used adjectively, with a
substantive; and their meaning may be exactly expressed by reversing the position of the elements of
the compound, and connecting them by one of the
prepositions *of, to,* and *for.* Thus, *death-bed,* bed
of death; *stumbling-block,* block of stumbling; *turning point,* point of turning; . . . But by no contri-
vance can we explain *stand-point* as the point of, or
to, or for, stand." [7]

In like fashion according to Richard Grant White
the following words are all to be rejected as illogically formed: *telegram, presidential, resurrected, re-
liable, practitioner, controversialist, conversationalist, agriculturalist, enthused, gubernatorial, ac-
countable, answerable.*

These views, that certain English words "are not
words" or are to be shunned because they are not
made according to some assumed rules and that all
uses of our words other than their so-called true and
correct meanings must be condemned, are so general
that they deserve to be examined in some detail in
the light of a few of the outstanding facts in the
history of our vocabulary.

What, for instance, are the facts concerning the
meaning of the word *nice?* This word came into the

[7] R. G. White, op. cit., pp. 232, 233.

English language not long after the Norman Conquest. It was borrowed directly from the French but is indeed the Latin word, *ne-scius*. The earliest meaning that we know for it is, therefore, *ignorant*. With this as a starting point the development in the idea conveyed by this word has been as follows: first *ignorant*, then *foolish*, then *trivial*, then *fastidious*, then *minutely discriminating*, *precise* or *accurate*, and then our common everyday use of the term *nice* to signify a *general approval*. Our purists insist that the last use is *incorrect*; that the *true* meaning of the word is only *minutely discriminating*, *precise*, or *accurate*. This judgment when viewed in the light of the various meanings through which the word has gone is practically asserting that the word *nice*, which originally meant *ignorant*, may legitimately pass through four changes but that its development must stop there; that it can correctly be used only in accord with the content it signified for a preceding age. One strongly suspects that the only reason they do not insist that the word *nice* must mean *ignorant* is the fact that they are usually unaware of its Latin derivation.

Even a most superficial reading of the older literature in our language reveals many changes in the meanings of words. A *villain* was formerly only a *farm-laborer*; a *knave* was originally a *boy*, later a *servant*; to *spill* was a general term meaning to *destroy* and had no special relation to liquids; so also *meat* was once *food* of any kind, not necessarily *flesh*. In the Old English rendering of the parable of the ten virgins five are described as *dizzy*. This word then meant *foolish,* and *silly* meant *blessed* or *good*. One could thus fill many pages recording only striking changes in the meanings of many words of our vocabulary. At once two practical questions arise. (a) How can one determine the meanings of words? and (b) Why cannot words be given definite meanings and keep those meanings without change?

The real meaning of any word must be finally determined, not by its original meaning, its source or etymology, but by the content given the word in actual present usage. The necessary dependence of language upon usage is more clearly seen in the matter of vocabulary than in the matters of grammar and pronunciation. In the case of words we realize at once that unless speaker and hearer attach the same content to a given signal there can be no communication. If, for instance, I decide to use the word *nice* as a tag for the idea *foolish* and assert that "John Smith is a *nice* man," most hearers would certainly fail to receive the idea that I mean a "*foolish* man." They would naturally take the word as a symbol for the idea of *general approval* which it usually represents in common usage. Even a hardy purist would scarcely dare pronounce a painter's masterpiece *awful,* without explanations.

As a social device for communication, language can fulfill its function only if the users of that language are agreed upon the symbols for ideas. There can thus be no meanings for words apart from usage.

At this point the second question arises. Why cannot we agree upon the meanings of our words, fix them, and prevent further changes? This is what Dr. Johnson first hoped to do when he planned his dictionary; after seven years of work on that dictionary, however, he writes:

"Those who have been persuaded to think well of my design, require that it should fix our language, and put a stop to those alterations which time and chance have hitherto been suffered to make in it without opposition. With this consequence I will confess I flattered myself for a while; but now begin to fear that I have indulged expectation which neither reason nor experience can justify. When we see men grow old and die at a certain time one after another, from century to century, we laugh at the elixir that promises to prolong life to a thousand years; and with equal justice may the lexicographer be derided, who, being unable to produce no example of a nation that has preserved their words and phrases from mutability, shall imagine that his dictionary can embalm his language, and secure it from corruption and decay, that it is in his power to change sublunary nature, or clear the world at once from folly, vanity and affectation. With this hope however, academies have been instituted, to guard the avenues of their languages, to retain fugitives, and repulse intruders: but their vigilance and activity have hitherto been vain; sounds are too volatile and subtile for legal restraints; to enchain syllables and to lash the wind, are equally the undertakings of pride, unwilling to measure its desires by its strength." [8]

To understand fully why words continually, although slowly, shift in meanings would be to realize the full relationship between language and experience. Here I can but touch, in the way of illustration, one or two aspects of the process of meaning or semantic change in words. I hope they may serve to establish the view that any language so long as it is living, so long as it is actually employed in the business of grasping and communicating experience in its fulness, must necessarily change and develop. An incident of baby-language that developed within one family will help make my point. A child not yet two years of age, attached the symbol *ow* to the meaning *hair*, evidently because whenever he pulled his father's hair there was the response *ow!* [au]. (It was an accustomed play for these two.) His

[8] Samuel Johnson, *Dictionary*, (1755), Preface.

mother's hair, his sister's hair, became *ow,* although they did not participate in the hair-pulling play. The family as a group took up and quite frequently substituted the word *ow* for the word *hair.* Later the boy suddenly spoke of grass as *ow.* He had noted a likeness and used the word *ow* to call attention to it. *Ow* was now used for both *grass* and *hair,* although its use for *hair* was less frequent. The final step came when the symbol *ow* was applied to the color *green* and for some time *ow* was the regular word for *green* in that family group.

This incident of word development was unusual only in respect to the short time within which the changes occurred, but that fact is accounted for by the smallness of the group using the word. The process seems fairly clear. Attention may center upon any one of many aspects of an experience named by a word and this word may then be used to grasp or communicate a new experience having this particular aspect as the only element in common. The word, *horn,* for instance, first signified the hard, pointed projections on the heads of certain hoofed animals. This word was then applied to those things which were made from the material of these horns: shoe-horn, powder-horn, lant-horn, etc. But one use of the *horn,* detached from the animal, was to produce a certain kind of sound. Attention shifted from the material to the sound and thus the word *horn* was applied to any instrument used to make this type of sound without regard to the material of which it was made. Most modern *horns* are of metal. But these instruments have points of similarity in shape. It is but natural, therefore, that a like shape should receive the same name, *horn*. We are continually trying to understand (analyze) and communicate experience. The procedure must necessarily be finding an attachment between the new and the old. As attention centers on differing aspects of objects (experiences) designated by words these words will inevitably shift in their meanings.

There are of course other extensions, transfers, and limitations of the meanings of words but the general principles of these changes are essentially similar. The word *head* as it applies to a part of the body is fairly definite. In speaking of the *head* of an army or the *head* of a valley one aspect of its relation to the body as a whole is in attention; in speaking of a *head* of cabbage an entirely different aspect serves as the connection. To *land* meant originally to pass from what was *not land* to what was. Attention has more and more been so centered *on the action itself* rather than its end that now one can speak of jumping from a rock and *landing* in the water. Unless one can contrive to prevent a shifting of the center of attention among the many aspects in which an object (experience) can be viewed he cannot prevent words from developing new content. The only *true* and *correct* meaning of a word, therefore, must be the particular content put into it by actual present usage. Arbitrarily to restore the earlier meanings of words is, from the nature of case, an impossibility.

It must also be obvious that, in as much as the content of words for us is dependent upon our experience with the objects they name, no words will have exactly the same expressive values for each person. The child, after much experience, learns to apply the word *dog* to the same particular class of animals as do his fellows. He accomplishes this result despite the fact that there is so great a variety of the characteristics of dogs that it is impossible to define just what makes up the concept to which we apply the term. Although the child attaches much the same denotative value to the word *dog* as do his companions, the associations of the word for him are an individual matter. If he has been bitten and frightened, the word *dog* brings with it unpleasant experiences; if he has had many hours of delightful play with a pet that he loves, the word *dog* gathers round itself associations of an entirely different character. Much of the feeling of dislike we have at times for certain words is due to such early experiences.[9] And in similar fashion words develop the rich expressive values that make literature possible.

The meanings for which a word stands we call its denotations; the associations which it suggests we call its connotations. Thus the common words, *father, mother, home, school, church,* have denotations that are more or less common to the users of our language, at least they converge; their connotations, however, differ from person to person and continually affect the content of the words. The use of words in a living language can never become simply a consideration of denotations; suggestions, associations, the connotations of words, must always be reckoned with. Even if some authorized academy could fix the denotations of words and prevent the natural development of meanings described in the preceding paragraphs, no authority could possibly control the connotations of words which also inevitably influence and cause changes in meanings.

From the discussion of the changing meanings of words one naturally passes to a consideration of other means by which a vocabulary grows and the criticisms that certain words are to be repudiated

[9] See F. N. Scott, *Verbal Taboos,* in *The Standard of American Speech and Other Papers,* pp. 165-190.

because they are illogically formed. Whenever individuals or a people attain to new ideas they need
new words. Frequently the new ideas come from
contacts with other races. Then quite naturally
the new conceptions bring with them their symbols from the foreign language. The borrowing of
words, therefore (by an individual as well as by a
people), is not only significant as a matter of vocabulary; it points to a growth in ideas. The immense Middle English borrowings from French, for
example, are clear evidence that the English people
of the thirteenth and fourteenth centuries were
then assimilating certain phases of French civiliza-
tion and culture, just as the sixteenth-century borrowings from Latin indicate a similar cultural assimilation of classical literature. Probably no one
now looks upon such borrowings as injurious to the
language; certainly our language could not afford
to give them up. It is, however, well for our present-day purists to understand that in many of their
objections to words they are continuing the attitude
toward the language, even if not the particular stric-
tures, of those who struggled against the borrowing
of foreign words.

"I am of this opinion that our tung should be
written cleane and pure, unmixt and unmangeled
with borowing of other tunges, wherein we take not

heed by tijm, ever borowing and never payeng, she shall be fain to keep her house as bankrupt." [10]

Among other methods by which the vocabulary of our language is being actively developed, two which give rise to a number of questions of acceptable English are the processes called *composition* and *functional change*. The first, composition, consists in joining together two meaning elements into a single word. Examples, which illustrate somewhat the diversity of the kinds of elements that are thus joined, are *railroad, typewriter, scarecrow, driveway, standpoint, downpour, output, evergreen, overdo, withstand, upon, alongside, already*. In compounds generally the tendency is toward the obscuring in pronunciation and thus a forgetting of the separate elements. As a result we have in modern English a great many words originally compounds which no longer appear as compounds either in form or in meaning. Thus *hussy* is from *hūs-wīf*, our modern *house-wife;* lord, from *hlāf-weard*, meaning "loafward"; *world* is *wer*, "man," and *œldu*, "age," meaning the "age of man"; *barn* is a combination of *ber*, "barley," and *œrn*, "building"; *stirrup* is *sty-rope* or "mounting rope."

Many times when part of a compound word has lost its significance for us, it has been altered to resemble some known meaning element even when the resulting combination would logically make no sense. *Sand-blind,* for example is a corruption of *sam-blind,* meaning "half blind"; *cutlass* is an attempt to English the French *coutelas* (Latin cultellus, "knife"). *Primrose* is not a compound with *rose,* nor is *belfry* related to *bell.* Both elements of *counter-pane* have been altered to sound like English words. In view of the great numbers of English words which now perpetuate *errors* of "folk etymologizing" it is futile to protest against a few that happen to have come to our attention. *Electrocute* and *electrocution* will remain useful words of our language despite the illogical nature of their formation, as will *ice-water* and *ice-cream.* The relations between the members of a compound word are of so many kinds that it seems impossible to exhaust the varieties. There is no more reason, therefore, to condemn *viewpoint* as illogical because it differs from some other combinations than to condemn the phrases "wireless operator" and "insane asylum" as illogical because the relation between the two words in each case differs fundamentally from that between the two words in the phrase "young man."

Another type of objection to certain compound words is equally futile. Some insist that only elements coming from the same language can properly be combined in a compound word.

"The word *racial* is an ugly word, the strangeness of which is due to our instinctive feeling that the termination *-al* has no business at the end of a word that is not obviously Latin." [11]

The word *tidal* is similarly disapproved, for here the Latin suffix *-al* is added to the English word *tide*. So also it is insisted that the Greek suffix *-ist*, should not be used in such words as *canoeist, typist, florist, educationalist, conversationalist*. Again the logical reasoning concerning this type of word formation could not possibly be applied consistently. To accept it as a principle of judgment would necessitate the rejection of hosts of words very generally accepted and used even by those who offer the criticism. A few of such hybrids which would have to be forbidden are: *because, around, outcry, overpower, unable, aimless, plentiful, falsehood, courtship, lifeguard, partake, bicycle, troublesome, heirloom*.

The other method of vocabulary development, functional change, although frequently condemned, is one of the most active processes in present-day English. The objection usually takes the form of demanding that words must remain the "part of speech" they have formerly been. In modern English, however, the lack of formal characteristics to distinguish "parts of speech" makes it particularly easy for the same word to fulfill several "func-

[11] Fowler and Fowler, *The King's English*, (1906), p. 22.

tions." Some will dispute our calling *store* an adjective in *a stone wall,* but they cannot refuse to call it a verb in the sentence "He will *stone* the dog." We may thus *down* our opponents and, in football, have three *downs. Feed* as a noun is usually accepted in such a phrase as *chicken feed;* in speaking of *a feed* it is frequently called slang. To *shoe* a horse, to *board* a ship, to *bridge* a gap, to *brown* the toast, are to most of us without reproach. One may not like *suicide* as a verb and he may object to the word *enthuse,* but to uphold as the reason for that objection the principle that words must not be used outside of their ordinary function would necessitate the rejecting of large numbers of vigorous expressions. Any attempt to apply such a principle presupposes the possibility of determining the *proper function* of the words of present-day English. I know of no criteria upon which to base such decisions apart from present-day usage, and certainly present usage should no more bind the future practice than the usage of Chaucer should furnish the laws for the present.

No discussion of English words from the point of view of acceptability can ignore the question of slang. In any approach to slang, however, one is immediately confronted with the primary difficulty of the whole problem, a definition. Just what is slang? Is Chaucer using slang when he says of the Monk,

> "He yaf nat of that text a pulled hen,
> That seith, that hunters been nat holy men;
> Ne that a monk, when he is cloisterlees,
> Is lykned til a fish that is waterlees;"

Or when he says of the Friar,

> "Un-to his ordre he was a noble post."

Is Shakespeare using slang in his 144th sonnet when he writes,

> "And whether that my angel be turn'd fiend
> Suspect I may, yet not directly tell;
> But being both from me, both to each friend,
> I guess one angel in another's hell:
> Yet this shall I ne'er know, but live in doubt,
> Till my bad angel fire my good one out."

The term *slang* has suffered such a wide extension of its signification during the last seventy-five years and has been applied to so many varieties of words that it is extremely difficult to draw the line between what is slang and what is not. The Century Dictionary says of it:

"Slang enters more or less into all colloquial speech and into inferior popular literature, as novels, newspapers, political addresses, and is apt to break out even in more serious writing. Slang as such is not necessarily vulgar or ungrammatical; indeed, ✓ it is generally correct in idiomatic form, and though frequently censured on this ground, it often, in fact, owes its doubtful character to other causes."

What are these "causes" to which slang owes its "doubtful character"?

Why should the expressions for certain ideas be called slang when we use Anglo-Saxon words, but not slang when we use for the same ideas the equivalent Latin words? Thus to call an objecting man *a kicker* is slang; to use the Latin equivalent *recalcitrant* is entirely acceptable. I use slang when I say that I *go for* a man or that I *jump on* him; but the Latin *assail,* or *assault,* or *insult* is free from any taint. I may ask one whether he *comprehends,* but to use the Anglo-Saxon equivalent, *catch on,* is slang.

In like fashion, the very same comparison or figure may be slang or not slang depending on the particular words used. To call a man *brazen* is not slang, but to say he has *brass* is, and therefore taboo. We may say one has *backbone* or *grit* and the figure is acceptable; it is slang to affirm that he has *nerve* or *sand*. He may be said to have the *face* to affirm his innocence but he cannot be said to have the *cheek* to do the same thing. The essential element of

slang, therefore, cannot lie in the ideas denoted by
the words.

Many clipped words are called slang; but there
are also many clipped words in the language which
are not now and never were slang. *Prof, doc, exam,
gent,* are unquestionably slang; *mob, bus, cab, cad,
wag, varsity, van, fence,* though formed in the same
way would hardly be called slang today. Certainly
no one could object to the following abbreviated
words: *piano, back, down, wayward, squire, size,
pose, puzzle, hoax.* The abbreviating of words,
therefore, is not necessarily using slang.

To take technical words out of their usual environment and apply them in a figurative way to
general situations has long been called slang. In
baseball, for instance, a man may be technically *off
his base* and it is perfectly legitimate to say so; to
carry this expression over to other situations and to
use it figuratively is slang. Similar phrases of a
technical origin are: *it is up to you, toe the mark,
a knock-out, well groomed;* to all of these in general
application many still object. The language is, however, full of vigorous expressions from similar
sources: "to *wrestle* with a problem," "to lose *track*
of an argument," "to cut goods *on the bias*," *fair
play, foul play, hazard, crestfallen.*

One can conclude, therefore:

(1) That the processes by which slang is formed

are only the legitimate language processes that are continually active within our vocabulary.

(2) That most slang owes its existence "to impatience with the constraint of ceremonious propriety of speech." It is very largely the language of revolt, and perhaps the only characteristic which is common to the various types of slang is this "flavor of forbidden fruit." Its connotations of humor and flippancy are thus more significant than the denotations of the symbols used.

(3) That, in view of the practical impossibility of today applying any measure by which definitely and acceptably we may distinguish slang from non-slang, we cannot reasonably take *any attitude toward slang in general*. The standards of acceptability must be applied to each individual case and can consistently be only those which we apply to all other classes of words in our vocabulary.

A brief statement of the principles which we can thus set up as standards of acceptable English in the matters of vocabulary will serve to draw to a conclusion the discussions of this chapter. We cannot escape the fact that words will gradually but inevitably change their meanings. Their significations cannot be finally determined and fixed. Whatever content, therefore, actual present usage puts into a word must be accepted as its real and correct meaning. The acceptability of any word must rest, not upon any consideration of its source, its former use, its relation to slang in general, the method of its formation, but solely upon the fitness of both its denotations and connotations for the idea which it is to express, for the occasion upon which it is used, and for the hearers or readers to whom it is addressed. The whole problem of "fitness" in language deserves considerable discussion, but it is a matter relating to the artistic view of language and must be reserved for treatment in the next chapter.

SELECTED REFERENCES

BARFIELD, OWEN, *History in English Words.*

BLOOMFIELD, LEONARD, *The Study of Language*, pp. 97-110.

BRÉAL, M. (trans. by Mrs. H. Cust) *Essai de Sémantique.*

EMERSON, O. F., *The History of the English Language*, Part III.

FOWLER, H. W., *A Dictionary of Modern English Usage.*

GREENOUGH, J. B. and KITTREDGE, G. L., *Words and Their Ways in English Speech;* (also Bibliography, Appendix 392-396).

HALL, J. LESLIE, *English Usage.*

JESPERSEN, OTTO, *Language, Its Nature, Development, and Origin,* Chapters VI, X, XI (pp. 208-215).

JESPERSEN, OTTO, *Philosophy of Grammar*, pp. 92-95.

KRAPP, G. P., *The English Language in America*, Vol. I, Chap. II.

KRAPP, G. P., *Modern English, Its Growth and Present Use*, Chapter VI.

LOUNSBURY, T. R., *The Standard of Usage in English*, Chap. VII.

MCKNIGHT, G. H., *English Words and Their Backgrounds*.

MATTHEWS, BRANDER, *Parts of Speech*, Chap. IV, V, VI, VII, VIII.

SAPIR, EDWARD, *Language*, Chapters II, IX.

SCOTT, F. N., *The Colloquial Nasals*, in *The Standard of American Speech and Other Papers*, pp. 272-278.

SCOTT, F. N., *Verbal Taboos*, in *Standard of American Speech and Other Papers*, pp. 165-190.

SKEAT, W. W., *Principles of English Etymology*, First and Second Series. (Technical in treatment.)

STURTEVANT, E. H., *Linguistic Change*, Chapters IV, V.

TRENCH, R. C. (Archbishop), *On the Study of Words*.

WEEKLY, ERNEST, *On Dictionaries*, in *Atlantic Monthly*, Vol. 133, pp. 782-791.

WEEKLEY, ERNEST, *The Romance of Words*.

WHITE, R. GRANT, *Words and Their Uses*.

American Speech (a monthly journal now in its second volume).

Dialect Notes (published by the American Dialect Society).

CHAPTER V

THE SCIENTIFIC AND THE ARTISTIC POINTS OF VIEW IN LANGUAGE

THE discussions of the preceding chapters have stressed the importance of the facts of usage in any consideration of standards of acceptable English. We have adopted as a fundamental principle the view that <u>usage is the final arbiter of all the correctness there can be in language</u>. As a practical program for the schools in their teaching we have suggested a limiting of their consideration to the particular usage of those who are carrying on the affairs of English-speaking people, because we have assumed that the education provided by the schools should bear directly upon and prepare for the affairs of life. But even from the point of view of a usage so limited there can be no narrow line distinguishing the acceptable from the unacceptable. Many conflicts and diversities appear in the practices of those in positions of influence and dignity, and there are many occasions upon which one is confronted with a considerable variety of language forms from which to choose. In the preceding chapters we have, therefore, addressed ourselves to the problem of setting up guiding principles to be used in these cases of divided usage; but we have urged throughout the exercise of a liberal tolerance when dealing with matters like grammar, pronunciation, and vocabulary. But somehow the idealist in us cannot fully acquiesce in any belief that holds up no view of a goal. Much as we condemn the purist's views and point to the ignorance with which he deals with the language we cannot help feeling that there may be something entirely valid behind his protests. It is this consideration which leads us to an attempt to bring together for examination and comparison the scientific and the artistic views of language.

It is the scientific attitude toward language which we have used in the discussions thus far and we have found it in opposition to many of the views commonly held by school teachers and the general public and expressed in the usual rules for correct English. The linguistic scientist begins by observing the external, objective facts of language. He wants a record of all the facts. He is primarily concerned with an attempt to classify these facts and, if possible, to account for them. With painstaking care he examines the language elements of all who use a given speech and he brings together all the evidence which will aid in establishing the earlier history of those language elements. He seems, at times, so preoccupied with establishing accurately minute matters in the early stages of the language that we are inclined to regard his interest and his efforts as entirely futile and utterly unrelated to life. To many of us the recording of the facts of the loss of final *n* in the inflections of early Middle English looks to be even less valuable than a game of checkers. But the scientist has learned that sound knowledge and understanding can rest only on a broad basis of established facts, and he knows that it is impossible to estimate in advance the importance of any fact. Time after time he has witnessed the overthrow of widely accepted theories and explanations which were too hastily reached and not honestly earned by patient investigation of all the facts. On the other hand he is aware of the increasing accumulations of the facts of his science and in his efforts to fill the gaps in those accumulations he knows that he is contributing to the historical perspective that must underlie any thoroughly sound understanding of language.

The linguistic scientist, therefore, is busy analyzing the sounds of language, tracing their development, questioning the causes of their changing. He investigates the circumstances under which words develop. He records and compares the formal patterns by which the symbols of a language have been and are related to convey meaning. And, like a true scientist, he is searching for pure knowledge. To know the facts and to understand language processes are to him ends in themselves. He leaves to others, usually, the engineering applications of the knowledge he has won. To judge the facts of language usage, to reduce them to a norm is not for him.

It is in part due to this detached interest of the scientific scholar of language that so little of the results of his investigations have influenced the practical teaching of the schools and the popular views and prejudices. A hundred years of linguistic scholarship based upon the historical method has had but little effect upon our inheritance of eighteenth-century language views.[1] It should be evident, however, that those who deal with language in a practical way, especially those who teach it, must look to the results of linguistic science for the knowledge upon which to base their procedure. This is by no means to say that the linguistic scientist is necessarily most competent to direct the applications of the contributions to knowledge which he produces. The use of scientific results in practical procedures is a special problem needing a scientific study all its own. But whether the linguistic scien-

[1] See Chapter I.

tist concerns himself about this special problem or not, those who do deal with the practical aspects of language must follow with understanding the results of linguistic research. Only in this way will they avoid the futile and even harmful practices that have resulted from ignorance. An adequate teaching of the English language must build its program upon essentially sound views of language processes and certainly cannot afford to rest upon those traditional ideas that modern linguistic science has shown to be false.

We cannot assume, however, that our linguistic science of today is by any means complete. Some of us feel, indeed, that in the scientific effort to be truly objective our linguistic scholars have not always recognized the great difference between their science and the so-called natural sciences. The parallel between the phenomena of language on the one hand and the facts of botany, or of geology, or of zoölogy, on the other is not fully satisfactory. In the natural sciences the facts, we believe, have a complete existence independent of human perceptions and thought.[2] The causes of change in the case of plant or animal life may be in the environment in which this life is placed but despite these

[2] For this practical discussion we are using the terms of popular language and avoiding the philosophical problem of reality. This language must not be interpreted as denying the conception of the "psychophysical continuum."

dependencies and relationships any particular specimen of plant or animal is in itself a complete functioning organism. The leaf, the blossom, the root, are in themselves objective facts for the science of botany. In language the situation is essentially different. The single sound, the unit of sound which we call the syllable, combinations of sounds, are also objective facts (external physical stimuli). But these sounds are not *facts of language* unless they are accompanied by the mental facts we call meaning. We may study vocal sounds by many scientific methods; we may photograph the vibrations of which they are composed, we may minutely analyze the muscular movements by which they are produced. But we are not studying *the facts of language* unless our study of these sounds includes the mental consequent produced by these sounds *in a linguistic community*. There is no *language* apart from a *mind* active in expression.[3]

[3] The word *expression* must be distinguished from *communication*. *Expression* is here used to signify the mental process of clearly grasping and formulating impressions.

"Every true intuition or representation is also *expression*. That which does not objectify itself in expression is not intuition or representation, but sensation and mere natural fact. . . . Intuitive activity *possesses intuitions to the extent that it expresses them*. . . . How can we really possess an intuition of a geometrical figure, unless we possess so accurate an image of it as to be able to trace it immediately upon paper or on the blackboard? . . . Every one can experience the internal illumination which follows upon his success in formulating to him-

Fundamentally, then, language is a tool of meaning. It is true that a leaf can be said to have meaning in respect to its function for the plant or in respect to its contributing to the perceived beauty of a bouquet, but as a leaf it is for man an external physical stimulus. A word is also for man an external physical stimulus in so far as it is a combination of sounds, but as a *word,* a language element, it is in addition a symbol functioning in a human mind analyzing experience. A satisfactory linguistic science, therefore, cannot confine itself to the so-called objective facts, the external physical stimuli; it must ultimately consider these objective facts from the point of view of the human function of language. Thought and language are so intimately bound up together that linguistic science cannot dispense with psychology. Without entering a discussion of this intricate relationship of language and thought we can state in brief fashion enough of that relationship to indicate something of the outlines of what must constitute a complete scientific view of language.

Several quotations will furnish a basis for our statements.

---

self his impressions and feelings, but only so far as he is able to formulate them. Feelings or impressions, then, pass by means of words from the obscure region of the soul into the clarity of the contemplative spirit." Croce, *Æsthetic,* (trans. Ainslie), pp. 8 and 9.

". . . any number of impressions, from any number of sensory sources, falling simultaneously on a mind which has not yet experienced them separately, will fuse into a single undivided object for that mind. The law is that all things fuse that can fuse, and nothing separates except what must. . . . The baby, assailed by eyes, ears, nose, skin, and entrails at once, feels it all as one great blooming, buzzing confusion; . . . A field of consciousness, however complex, is never analyzed unless some of its ingredients have changed. We *now discern,* 'tis true, a multitude of coexisting things about us every moment: but this is because we have had a long education, and each thing we now see distinct has been already differentiated from its neighbors by repeated appearances in successive order. To the infant, sounds, touches, and pains, form probably one unanalyzed bloom of confusion. . . . In general, then, if an object affects us simultaneously in a number of ways, *abcd,* we get a peculiar integral impression, which thereafter characterizes to our mind the individuality of that object, and becomes the sign of its presence; and which is only resolved into *a, b, c, d,* respectively by the aid of further experiences. . . . If any single quality or constituent, *a,* of such an object, have previously been known by us isolatedly, or have in any other manner already become an object of separate acquaintance on our part, so that we have an image of it, distinct or vague, in our mind, disconnected with *bcd,* then that constituent *a* may be analyzed out from the total impression. Analysis of a thing means separate attention to each of its parts. . . . Only such elements as we are acquainted with, and can imagine, separately, can be discriminated within a total sense-impression." [4]

To this view of the developing analysis of experience must be joined the following statement from John Dewey:

"The chief intellectual classifications that constitute the working capital of thought have been built up for us by our mother tongue. Our very lack of explicit consciousness in using language that we are employing the intellectual systematizations of the race shows how thoroughly accustomed we have become to its logical distinctions and groupings. . . . Since intellectual life depends on possession of a store of meanings, the importance of language as a tool of preserving meanings cannot be overstated." [5]

Leonard Bloomfield sums up the situation clearly in a brief paragraph:

"Every experience is composed of a number of elements whose individuality is due to their having occurred in other contexts in past experiences. Thus we have seen the color of the rabbit, other four-footed animals, other running animals, and the like.

[4] William James, *Principles of Psychology*, Vol. 1, pp. 488, 495, 503.

[5] John Dewey, *How We Think*, pp. 175, 174.

Each element recalls those past experiences in which it figured. But it does this obscurely, until language has given the experience a fixed and easily handled symbol with which we can keep it from slipping, as it were, through our fingers. Once language exists, however, the analysis of the experience into these elements is bound to develop. At least it takes place in all known languages and is in all of them, as time goes on, being perfected by a gradual but unceasing process of development, to which we must ascribe also its origin." [6]

"The development of language, accordingly, must have advanced in inseparable connection with that of the mental powers generally." [7]

To put it briefly, the scientific study of language, therefore, must start with and rest upon the records of the linguistic habits of a community. It attempts to gather all the facts, to classify them, and to account for them. It has as its goal the formulating of the laws in accordance with which language behaves; in other words it aims to arrive at a complete understanding of language processes. In this effort, scientific study cannot confine its observations to the so-called objective data of sounds and forms and grammatical apparatus for these sounds and forms are *language* only as they function for man in his intellectual struggle to under-

[6] Leonard Bloomfield, *The Study of Language*, p. 57.
[7] Leonard Bloomfield, op. cit., p. 56.

stand and communicate experience. Any thorough study of linguistic phenomena must take account of the human origin and purpose of language. It may indeed be true that there are language developments and changes which can be accounted for solely on the basis of the external physical characteristics of the language facts. One is inclined to believe, however, that the dynamic of most language changes is to be found in the struggle of a linguistic community to carry out a complete analysis of experience. In no language is such an analysis perfected. Some languages stress categories to which others pay no attention. Our language, for example, sees actions always in relation to a present, past, or future time; some languages ignore the matter of time and consider only whether the action is complete or incomplete. The recognizing of new relationships, new likenesses, new differences, is continually registering itself in deviations of language usage.

The following brief quotation will not only serve to restate this point but will also lead us to our next consideration, the artistic point of view in language:

"Everything that we have thus far seen to be true of language points to the fact that it is the most significant and colossal work that the human spirit has evolved—nothing short of a finished form of expression for all communicable experience. This form may be endlessly varied by the individual without thereby losing its distinctive contours; and it is constantly reshaping itself as is all art. Language is the most massive and inclusive art we know, a mountainous and anonymous work of unconscious generations." [8]

The artistic view of language can perhaps best be approached by attempting to state in broad outline the artistic purpose. In general I conceive art as an effort to satisfy the yearning of the human mind and spirit to experience all of life to the full and to arrest and contemplate that experience. For this purpose all art is expression.

"Apart from expression, experience may be vivid and satisfactory as we feel and think and dream and act; yet it is always in flux, coming and going, shifting and unaware. But through expression it is arrested by being attached to a permanent form, and there can be retained and surveyed. Experience, which is otherwise fluent and chaotic, or when orderly too busy with its ends to know itself, receives through expression the fixed, clear outlines of a thing, and can be contemplated like a thing. Every one has verified the clarifying effect of expression upon ideas, how they thus acquire definiteness and coherence so that even the mind that thinks them can hold them in review. But this effect upon feeling is no less sure. The unexpressed values of

[8] Edward Sapir, *Language*, p. 235.

experience are vague strivings embedded in chaotic
sensations and images; these expression sorts and
organizes by attaching them to definite ordered symbols. Even what is most intimate and fugitive becomes a stable object. When put into patterned
words the subtlest and deepest passions of a poet,
which before were felt in a dim and tangled fashion,
are brought into the light of consciousness. In
music, the most elusive moods, by being embodied
in ordered sounds, remain no longer subterranean,
but are objectified and lifted into clearness. In the
novel or drama, the writer is able not only to enact
his visions of life in the imagination, but, by body-
ing them forth in external words and acts, to possess them for reflection. In painting, all that is seen
and wondered at in nature is seen with more deli-
cacy and discrimination and felt with greater freedom; or the vague fancies which a heated imagination paints upon the background of a mind come
out more vivid and better controlled, when put
with care upon a canvas.

"Even ordinary conversation, of course, arrests
and clarifies experience, enabling us to commune
with ourselves; but since its purpose is usually beyond itself, this result is hasty and partial, limited
to what is needful for the practical end in view. In
art alone is this value complete. For there, life is
intentionally held in the medium of expression, put
into color and line and sound for the clear sight and
contemplation of men. The aim is just to create
life upon which we may turn back and reflect." [9]

[9] DeWitt H. Parker, *The Principles of Æsthetics*, pp. 37, 38.

The artist then would carry a keen sensitiveness into every part of existence and then strive to crystallize and socialize his experience by some means of expression. To satisfy him, the medium of expression must fully and accurately realize the experience. Thus Masefield's *Dauber:*

" 'Even as he spoke his busy pencil moved,
    Drawing the leap of water off the side
    Where the great clipper trampled iron-hooved,
    Making the blue hills of the sea divide,
    Shearing a glittering scatter in her stride,
    And leaping on full tilt with all sails drawing,
    Proud as a war-horse, snuffing battle, pawing.

" 'I cannot get it yet—not yet,' he said;
    'That leap and light, and sudden change to green,
    And all the glittering from the sunset's red,
    And the milky colours where the bursts have been,
    And then the clipper striding like a queen
    Over it all, all beauty to the crown.
    I see it all, I cannot put it down.

" 'It's hard not to be able. There, look there!
    I cannot get the movement nor the light;
    Sometimes it almost makes a man despair
    To try and try and never get it right.
    Oh, if I could—oh, if I only might,
    I wouldn't mind what hells I'd have to pass,
    Not if the whole world called me fool and ass.' " [10]

[10] John Masefield, *Dauber*, lines 64-84.

When, then, the artist turns to language as his medium of expression he approaches it from the practical point of view. He begins with vivid experience which he tries to grasp and possess completely through the expressive values of language symbols. All too frequently his impressions "break through language and escape" and the expression is therefore *ugly* rather than *beautiful*.

"The individual A is seeking the expression of an impression which he feels or anticipates, but has not yet expressed. See him trying various words and phrases which may give the sought-for expression, that expression which must exist, but which he does not possess. He tries the combination *m*, but rejects it as unsuitable, inexpressive, ugly: He tries the combination *n*, with a like result. He does not see at all, or does not see clearly, the expression still eludes him. After other vain attempts, during which he sometimes approaches, sometimes retreats from the mark at which he aims, all of a sudden (almost as though formed spontaneously of itself) he forms the sought-for expression, and *lux facta est*. He enjoys for an instant æsthetic pleasure or the pleasure of the beautiful. The ugly, with its correlative displeasure, was the æsthetic activity which had not succeeded in conquering the obstacle; the beautiful is the expressive activity which now displays itself triumphant." [11]

[11] Benedetto Croce, *Æsthetic*, (trans. Ainslie), p. 118.

To the artistic point of view, therefore, beauty of language does not consist in decorations or ornament; it does not rest in sounds or syllables or any particular language forms; it is not a matter of pronunciation, or grammar, or vocabulary, as such; it is to be measured by the fulness of realization which attends the language symbols used. The artist is forever unsatisfied with the crudities and failures of incomplete representation. He demands of language that it catch and communicate meanings in delicate shades of discrimination; that it function with "the same associative effectiveness that the original object would have"; [12] that it realize an idea, or an event, or a feeling, in all the light and shadow that was present in the initial vivid experience.

There are some who would strive for the artist's "beauty of language" by means of recipes and rules and formulas dealing with the externals of language. But beauty can never be won on such terms. It is no more possible to secure it by changing one's pronunciation of certain vowels, by refraining from slang, by adhering to formal grammatical rules, than it is to make one a gentleman by clothing him in a dress suit or to become a plumber by acquiring overalls and a kit of tools. There can be no satisfying beauty of linguistic forms apart from the use of

[12] H. L. Hollingworth, *The Psychology of Thought*, p. 207.

these forms in the function of language to mediate experience.

Nor can we justly set off the artistic approach to language as something belonging to a narrow group or cult. We must not view the artist's purpose as essentially different in kind from the practical language purposes of the ordinary man. The difference is one of degree, not of nature. The ordinary man, like the artist, receives the impressions of experience; he also needs a medium through which to grasp, to possess, to communicate these impressions; he likewise uses language for these needs of expression. To be sure he may be less sensitive to impressions; he may be less keen in his realizations, and he is usually satisfied with a more crude and inaccurate representation. But his object in the practical use of language is part of the same purpose which controls the artist (he may be less conscious of his purpose and his tools) and the measure of success must be the same in both cases—vivid realization and complete representation.

". . . the principal reasons which have prevented Æsthetic, the science of Art, from revealing the true nature of art, its real roots in human nature, has been its separation from the general spiritual life, the having made of it a sort of special function or aristocratic club. No one is astonished when he learns from physiology that every cell is an organism

and every organism a cell or synthesis of cells. No
one is astonished at finding in a lofty mountain the
same chemical elements that compose a small stone
fragment. There is not one physiology of small animals and one of large animals; nor is there a special
chemical theory of stones as distinct from moun-
tains. In the same way, there is not a science of
lesser intuition as distinct from a science of greater
intuition, nor one of ordinary intuition as distinct
from artistic intuition. There is but one Æsthetic,
the science of intuitive or expressive knowledge,
which is the æsthetic or artistic fact. And this
Æsthetic is the true analogue of Logic, which includes, as facts of the same nature, the formation of
the smallest and most ordinary concept and the most
complicated scientific and philosophical system." [13]

When one brings into one view the scientific and
the artistic approaches to language he finds no
fundamental conflict, as is sometimes assumed. He

[13] Benedetto Croce, *Æsthetic*, (trans. Ainslie), p. 14.
In connection with this quotation one may question my failure
to distinguish between the use of language for artistic purposes
and the use of language for scientific purposes. I should insist,
however, that the language process is fundamentally the same
in both cases. In both there is the attempt to *express* experience
fully, accurately, vividly. In the artistic purpose the attention
centers on the individual aspects of the impressions, the immediate intuitive experience; in the scientific purpose the attention is carried away from the individual aspects of the experience
to significant relationships. Thus the scientist frequently uses
formal symbols (algebraic or chemical signs) in order to free
his thinking from the interference of extraneous or irrelevant
associations and center it upon the abstract relationships.

finds, rather, two complementary attitudes which together will provide the principles of a sound constructive program of teaching the English language.

The artistic view is the practical approach. From this point of view language is a means to an end, and that end is specifically to grasp, to possess, to communicate experience. Accordingly, that is good language, good English, which, on the one hand, most fully realizes one's impressions, and, on the other, is most completely adapted to the purposes of any particular communication.[14] The artistic motive thus furnishes the dynamic of most language change and development. We may even insist that a language progresses as it develops possibilities of a more and more complete analysis of human experience. This therefore that we have described as the artistic purpose, furnishes us both our definition of *good* English and the ultimate goal in the teaching of the English language in our schools.

The recognition of this artistic purpose as the objective of our language teaching implies the subordination of our attention to the externals of language forms. The significance of conforming to the speech forms of any particular dialect will be discussed in the next chapter. It is enough here to

[14] A discussion of the larger problems of communication is not included here but is reserved for a forthcoming book entitled *The Teaching of English Composition.*

ısist that we must not mistake any such external
onformity with the speech habits of a particular
lialect as identical with good or artistic or beau-
iful English.

In the scientific view of language the artistic pur-
ɔose is recognized as one of the fundamental facts
ɔf language and it must be accepted as furnishing
at least one of the "whys" of language change. The
scientific student sets himself to understand the ways
in which language operates to fulfill its human
function. The scientific study of language processes
and laws, therefore, provides the knowledge necessary to guide our practical procedures in the teaching of language. Only by using to the full the
results of scientific linguistic study will our teaching avoid the futile and injurious practices of some
of our traditional methods and make possible unmistakable progress toward good English.

It will be the purpose of the next three chapters
to try to make definite the implications of these
principles for a practical program in the schools.

SELECTED REFERENCES

BLOOMFIELD, LEONARD, *The Study of Language,* Chap.
    III, IV (73-97), VIII.
CROCE, BENEDETTO, *Æsthetic* (trans. Ainslie), Chap. I,
    II, III, IX, XIII, XVI, XVIII.
DEWEY, JOHN, *How We Think,* Chapters IX, XIII.

EASTMAN, MAX, *The Enjoyment of Poetry*.

HOLLINGWORTH, H. L., *The Psychology of Thought*.

JESPERSEN, OTTO, *Language, Its Nature, Development and Origin*, Preface, Chap. XIV, XV, and Book IV.

MASEFIELD, JOHN, *Dauber*.

PARKER, DEWITT H., *The Principles of Æsthetics*, Chap II, III, IV, X.

PILLSBURY, W. B., *The Psychology of Reasoning*, Chap V.

PILLSBURY, W. B., *The Reading of Words*, in *American Journal of Psychology*, Vol. VIII, pp. 315-393.

SAPIR, EDWARD, *Language*, Chap. IX, X, XI.

SCOTT, F. N., *The Genesis of Speech*, in *The Standard of American Speech and Other Papers*, pp. 312, 345.

STEVENSON, R. L., *On Style in Literature*, in *Contemporary Review*, Vol. 47, pp. 548-561.

STEVENSON, R. L., *A College Magazine*.

STURTEVANT, E. H., *Linguistic Change*, Chap. VII, VIII.

WHITMAN, WALT, *An American Primer*.

WUNDT, WILLIAM, *Elements of Folk Psychology* (trans. Schaub), pp. 53-75.

CHAPTER VI

THE PROBLEMS OF THE TEACHER: DEVELOPING HABITS

NOT long ago I visited a high school class in English literature in one of the larger mid-Western cities. During the recitation one of the boys, Henry, spoke enthusiastically about a book by Robert Louis Stevenson that he had been reading. In the course of his talk he twice used the expression *had wrote*. After the boy had finished, the teacher proceeded to correct his English. She said, "Henry, give us the principal parts of the verb *write*." He recited correctly, "Present infinitive, *to write*, past tense, *wrote*, past participle, *written*." Then she said, "Now, Henry, conjugate the verb *write* in the past-perfect tense." Again, although he looked somewhat bewildered, he satisfactorily gave the required forms. Finally the teacher said, "In your talk just now you must have spoken without thinking, for you said *had wrote* instead of *had written*."

Now, as a matter of fact, *to speak without thinking of the forms of language* is exactly what the boy should have done. If he is to speak effectively he must give his entire attention to grasping clearly his ideas and to the choice and organization of the materials underlying those ideas in order to meet the needs of his hearers. Language forms, the grammatical apparatus of his expression, must come automatically. Just as a child can be said to have learned to walk only when the act of balancing and the placing of his feet in steps have become unconscious processes, so he has really learned a language only when the grammatical forms of that language have become habits.

"Language is not a process of logical reference to a conscious set of rules; the process of understanding, speaking and writing is everywhere an associative one. Real language-teaching consists, therefore, of building up in the pupil those associative habits which constitute the language to be learned." [1]

One must add, therefore, another requisite of good or beautiful English to those we have already given in the preceding chapter. It is not enough that the language must thoroughly fit, in both denotation and suggestion, the ideas, the occasion, and the needs of the hearers; it must also be *used with freedom*. Good driving of an automobile cannot be accomplished so long as the driver must think of

[1] Leonard Bloomfield, *The Study of Language*, p. 294.

each separate movement necessary to start the car, to change gears, to increase or to diminish speed, to steer a straight line or to negotiate a corner, to stop. It is only when all these processes have become so automatic that they are carried out unconsciously in accord with the general desires motivating the driving that one has really learned and is on the way to good driving. In language teaching, therefore, the outstanding problem is the developing of habits.

But the pupils who come to us in the schools have already acquired a set of habits in English. They all use the English language with some degree of efficiency. They can communicate quite satisfactorily with the members of their own families or with their daily companions in their neighborhood. The first problem of the English teacher is to determine what new habits in English language, if any, these pupils should acquire. Before answering such a question, however, one must understand something of the significance of differing habits within the English language. One must realize, for instance, that there are necessarily differences in language habits ranging in degree all the way from the minute individual peculiarities which enable us to distinguish the voice of a friend over the telephone, through those greater divergencies which make it difficult to understand a north-county Englishman, to such totally strange linguistic practices as characterize the native speech of a Chinaman. Most of us cannot communicate with the Turk who knows only his own language, simply because we have one set of language habits and he another. The various so-called dialects within a language are only differing sets of language habits that come nearer to a single norm than do those of two separate languages.[2] We can thus use the term *dialect* for any distinct set of language habits whether they are matters of pronunciation, of grammar, of vocabulary, or of all three combined. Our question becomes then an inquiry as to what set of language habits, what dialect of English, the schools should try to develop in the pupils.

We are all familiar with some of the differences between the pronunciation of a native of Georgia and that of a native of eastern Massachusetts. We know that the pronunciation of the Middle West differs from both of these. Is it the business of the schools of Georgia to seek to develop in their pupils the pronunciation habits that are current in Boston or in Chicago? Such an attempt would be thoroughly futile not only because it would be impossible to accomplish, but because there would be no real advantage secured for those pupils even if it could be accomplished, to say nothing of the neglect of

[2] See note No. 1 of Chapter II.

matters of really vital importance. It is quite true that these native pronunciation habits will convey to hearers the connotation that the speaker comes from the South, but certainly that suggested information is entirely desirable. It is surely as acceptable to come from Georgia as it is to come from Boston or Chicago and there can be no real gain from any attempt to develop at great effort pronunciation habits that would conceal the fact. In similar fashion there are in the various sections of our country distinctive habits of vocabulary and of grammar. Such linguistic practices, the distinctive language habits of separate sections of the English-speaking world, are the so-called *geographical dialects* of English. It is clearly not the business of the schools in any one of these sections to teach the language habits which constitute the dialect of another section, for the general speech practices of the Middle West are just as good as those of New England, and the Southerners have long been justly proud of their dialect.

But, says the objector, is there not a *standard* English language that is approximately the same in all sections of the country? At this point one must distinguish between written English and spoken English. There is a *literary* English, the language of books, that is fairly uniform over the whole English-speaking world. Of course, there are different levels of literary English, ranging from the very formal structure and vocabulary of extremely serious books to the conversational structure and easy-going vocabulary of informal publications. In the more informal materials a greater number of the differences in language habits characteristic of geographical dialects show themselves. It is, however, approximately accurate to say that the local differences of formal literary language are for practical purposes almost negligible. If, then, we are concerned with developing *in the writing* of our pupils the habits of formal literary language, there can be little question about the set of habits to be chosen. We should follow the language practices current in the books recently written and published. We must, however, realize that the habits of *written language* are not those of the *spoken language,* and that they must be definitely developed for writing and in connection with writing. The decision as to how far the schools should go in the matter of striving to equip all students with the writing language habits of formal literary discourse must rest upon a consideration of the values of those habits of written language for the particular students concerned.[3]

---

[3] We must not confuse the problem of developing *in writing certain language habits* with the problem of developing the *ability to communicate effectively by means of writing.* The second problem can never be solved by an attack on the first. Effective communication is more than a matter of language

Certainly, from a practical point of view, the habits of written language are, for the great mass of pupils, considerably less important than their habits of spoken English.

Someone may urge, however, that we teach our pupils to use in *their speech* this dialect of literary written English which appears in approved books. Our schools have frequently adopted this view and teachers have attempted the utterly impossible task of making the pupil "talk like a book." One reason that the schools have made but little impression on the language used by the pupil outside the classroom lies in the fact that the English taught is not the *informal spoken English* of everyday life. No one who is a good speaker of English in the conversational situations that make up so many of our occasions to use the language, uses entirely the grammatical structure and the vocabulary of formal literary English. Of course in some respects the forms and structure of the two sets of language habits overlap, but we must recognize that in neither grammar nor vocabulary are literary written English and spoken English identical. If one ignores the differences of geographical dialects the situation may be roughly represented by the following diagram.

---

habits and is the central problem of English composition. It is therefore not discussed in this book.

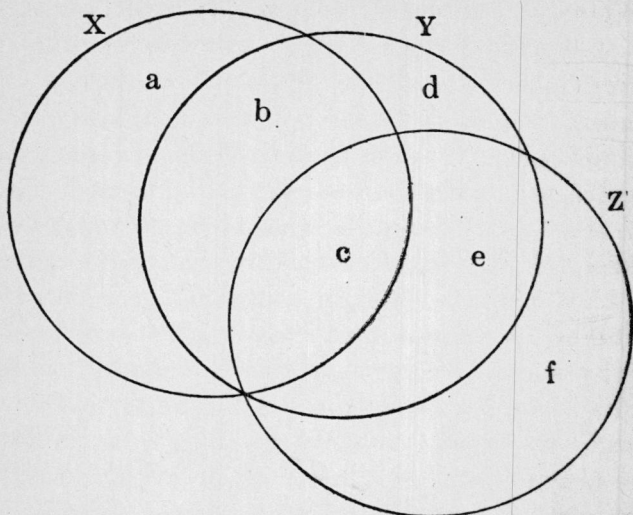

The three circles X, Y, Z represent the three dialects—the three sets of speech habits—referred to in this chapter.

X—formal literary English, the forms and syntax that one finds in serious books.

Y—informal spoken English, of the socially accepted group.

Z—"vulgar" English, the speech of the illiterate whose native language is English.

Segments b, c, and e represent the overlappings of the three types of English.

c—that which is common to all three: formal literary English, the informal spoken English of the socially accepted group, and "vulgar" English.

b—that which is common to both formal literary English and the informal spoken English of the socially accepted group.

e—that which is common to both the informal spoken English of the socially accepted group and to "vulgar" English.

Segments a, d, and f represent those portions of each set of habits that are peculiar to the particular dialect.

We may justly insist, therefore, that the particular speech habits with which our teaching must concern itself should be those of conversational English. We do find, however, that in this conversational spoken English there are not only the differences that make our so-called geographical dialects but also differences within the communities themselves which mark what are sometimes called the *class dialects*. Roughly speaking, it is indeed true that the various social classes within any community maintain somewhat different sets of speech habits. One must hasten to emphasize in this connection the words "roughly speaking," for in the typical American community there are not easily distinguished lines of division between social classes and there is little difficulty in the passing from one social class to another. Nevertheless there are the speech habits which characterize those who have been members of the socially acceptable group and other speech habits that mark those who have lacked such associations.

The differences between these two social groups are evident not only in matters of speech, but also generally in matters of dress, in occupations, and in social manners. Just as overalls and calloused, grimy hands suggest a laboring man, or a well-made, neatly fitting dress suit, soft hands, and courtly manners suggest the best "society," so the speech

habits in which occur such expressions as "I seen my
mistake as soon as I done it" will suggest the characteristics of those who have lacked certain social
contacts. In any consideration of the different sets
of speech habits the matter of greatest significance
is this fact that speech not only functions for communication but also suggests, as do other modes of
social behavior, whatever characteristics usually ac-
company the language forms used.

In the light of this statement concerning differences in speech habits, one may criticize three of
the commonplaces frequently urged concerning our
language. First, it is often maintained that the
speech habits of the socially acceptable are *correct*
and that those of the other groups are *incorrect*.
From the point of view we have here set forth concerning differing dialects we are driven to the conclusion that such a judgment is untenable. There
is a correctness in each of the dialects. One speaks
correctly the dialect of the socially acceptable when
he uses accurately the speech habits common to that
group; he speaks it incorrectly when, while pretend-
ing to use those speech habits, he introduces language forms not practiced by that particular group.
Likewise, one speaks the dialect of "vulgar" [4] Eng-

---

[4] The word "vulgar" is here used to refer to the unschooled
or unlettered common man; it must not be taken to mean coarse
or offensive to good taste.

lish correctly when he uses accurately the speech habits of those whose language it is; he speaks "vulgar" English incorrectly when he introduces language forms not current in that dialect. Because many of the language forms and patterns are similar in the several social dialects of English and because our democratic society allows for only partial exclusiveness, the chances of dialect mixture are many. It is indeed always a question whether a democratic society can afford to permit a class consciousness of any kind to develop, especially a class consciousness based on language differences.

Second, it is frequently assumed that the dialect of "vulgar" English is *easy,* and that the dialect of the socially acceptable is more difficult. Accordingly the substitution of language forms from "vulgar" English into the latter dialect is called *careless* speech. The truth of the matter is that either dialect is equally *easy* to those whose *native* speech it is and the other dialect is about equally difficult to the one who tries to substitute it for his own. To substitute the language forms of one's native dialect for those of another dialect which we are attempting to use signifies that the new dialect is still imperfectly mastered. To use "I saw" and "I did" in speaking "vulgar" English is just as incorrect and careless as to use "I seen" and "I done" in the dialect of the socially acceptable.

It is frequently true also that the language forms found in "vulgar" English are remnants from an older stage of the language. In these matters "vulgar" English is more conservative than the dialect of the socially acceptable. For example, the double negative in such an expression as "They *didn't* take *no* oil with them" is a clinging to a mode of expression which reaches back more than a thousand years. In the parable of the ten virgins as it is rendered in the Anglo-Saxon Gospels the language is "ond nĕ nāmon nanne ele mid him." In Old English as in Classical Greek double negatives provided the normal way to express a strong negation. Chaucer's description of the knight is familiar. A literal rendering of his language in Modern English would be "He never yet no unfit speech didn't say in all his life unto no kind of man." In the case of the double negative the dialect of the socially acceptable group has made a change in practice while "vulgar" English perpetuates the older usage. In similar fashion the so-called double comparison in "more hotter" and the so-called double superlative in "most unkindest" harks back to the time when *more* and *most* were not yet the function words of comparison displacing the inflections. The use of *clomb* (usually spelled *clumb* when represented in writing) as the past tense form of *climb*, as "They clomb [klʌm] up the tree," is older than *climbed*. The dialect of he socially acceptable has allowed the verb *climb* o go over to the regular pattern of the weak verbs vhile "vulgar" English has kept the older and more difficult form. In the case of *ourn, hisn, theirn,* vulgar" English has used the pattern of the *-n* endngs in *mine* and *thine,* the older model; the other lialect has used the pattern of the genitive *-s* ending vhich originally belonged to certain classes of nouns.

One could fill pages with examples to prove that n many respects "vulgar" English is more conservative than other social dialects, and, if anything, more difficult because of its perpetuating exceptional forms. The common idea that "vulgar" English is a degenerate form derived by carelessness from the dialect of the socially acceptable is entirely without foundation. On the other hand, a few of the distinct usages of "vulgar" English illustrate a more complete carrying out of changes begun early and only partly carried out in other dialects. Thus, for example, the excrescent *t* on *once* and *twice* is only applying further the same sound additions that have already been accepted for *against, interest, midst.* The form appearing in *drownded* is historically parallel with the form *sounded.* Both originally had no *d* following the *n.*

Third, it is frequently maintained that the language forms in the speech habits of those who are socially acceptable are more beautiful than the forms which appear in "vulgar" English. It is difficult to argue such a question, for I know of no satisfactory standard of beauty or artistic excellence other than the one given in the preceding chapter. I suspect, however, that careful analysis would show that the deficiencies in beauty which many feel in respect to the language forms of "vulgar" English have no relation whatever to the objective qualities of the forms themselves but are due to the fact that these language forms inevitably, though perhaps not very consciously, suggest the characteristics of the people we know who use "vulgar" English. The language forms, aside from their communicative value, redintegrate [5] the circumstances of the situation in which we have frequently heard them. When these circumstances are unpleasant we naturally dislike the language forms that call them up.

We are now ready to give a more direct answer to the question, raised early in this chapter, as to what set of language habits, what dialect of English,

[5] "It is a simple process, which we are, however, inclined to call by a formidable name—redintegration. A part of a complex stimulus, recurring by itself or in some foreign context, provokes a complete reaction previously made to the total situation of which this detail was a part. . . . The fundamental fact underlying all these associative processes is perhaps the tendency for brain patterns to be reinstated more or less completely when any of their parts are excited."
H. L. Hollingworth, *The Psychology of Thought*, pp. 92, 94.

the schools should seek to develop in the pupils.
Whether for good or ill, the schools seem to be com-
mitted to the program of equipping the pupils with
the language habits of those we have called the
socially acceptable group. This program is defensible on the ground that the schools are preparing
pupils to take part intelligently in the affairs of our
communities, and there is no doubt that this social
dialect is the one most used in the management of
those affairs. This program, however, is defensible
only if it is accompanied by an intelligent attitude
toward language and if the dialect is liberally viewed.

In accord with such a program it is the business
of the English teacher first to analyze the speech
habits of the particular pupils in his classes. In
this connection we must give passing attention to
the several attempts already made to determine such
a language program for the schools. My criticisms
upon these efforts will, negatively at least, aid in
clarifying the reasons for the procedure suggested
here. Four such attempts demand brief comment.
Professor W. W. Charters has brought together [6]
the studies of "the language errors of school children" in order to construct a language curriculum
of the particular habits which these children need
to master. In his own words ". . . it is apparent

[6] *The Sixteenth Yearbook* of the Society for the Study of
Education, Part I, pp. 85-110.

that the first step is to ascertain the rules which are broken and to determine their relative importance." As a method of determining the particular language habits which the schools should teach this approach seems unsatisfactory for three reasons:

(1) It assumes as the infallible measures of correctness the grammar rules which we have shown above (Chapter I) to be untrustworthy.

(2) It proceeds upon the principle that the more frequent a so-called error the more important it is to eradicate it. There is no consideration for the fact that the greater the frequency, the nearer it may be to the actual usage of the socially acceptable, and there is no attempt to see the significance of the so-called errors in respect to the historical development of the language.

(3) Even if we can ignore the fact that errors of spelling, punctuation, paragraphing, unity, coherence, "ambiguous reference," "monotony" and courtesy are all indiscriminately included as "language" errors, we cannot use a study that makes no effort to separate the matters of formal literary written English from the matters of informal spoken English.

Much the same criticisms can be applied to the work of Stormzand and O'Shea,[7] although their at-

[7] Stormzand and O'Shea, *How Much English Grammar?* (1924).

tempt to evaluate the particular items of a grammar program in terms of frequency of use as well as frequency of error is a reaching out toward a safer measure of importance.

The recent study by Thorndike *et al.*,[8] attempting to inventory English constructions and to estimate their relative importance in the language by means of statistical methods, applies only to literary written English and not to the spoken English with which we are here concerned. Even from the point of view of written English this study suffers not only because it includes as "constructions" logical and vocabulary matters as well as grammatical forms but especially from the fact that the constructions are analyzed in accord with an apparatus that belongs to an older formal rather than the newer scientific grammar.

The fourth study by Leonard and Moffatt[9] is much more helpful as far as it goes. It is a genuine effort to place in respect to the social dialects of English about a hundred expressions that are frequently condemned by teachers. Its conclusions rest upon the observations and opinions of a picked group and, in lieu of a scientific record of the actual

[8] Edward L. Thorndike and Others, *An Inventory of English Constructions with Measures of Their Importance*, in Teachers College Record, Vol. XXVIII, pp. 580-610, (February, 1927).

[9] Leonard and Moffatt, *Levels in English Usage*, in The English Journal, Vol. XVI, pp. 345-359, (May, 1927).

facts of usage, it furnishes a fairly satisfactory guide concerning a rather large number of the troublesome matters of speech.

We have at hand, therefore, no satisfactory apparatus which will furnish a complete guide to the teacher who sets out to analyze the speech habits of his pupils. There has never been an adequate scientific survey of the spoken language in English and the teacher must depend upon his own observation and such aids as linguistic science can now furnish. In some communities he will find that the speech habits of most of his pupils are in accord with those of the dialect of the socially acceptable. In such a case there is for him practically no problem of developing *new* speech habits in his pupils but he may pass at once to the matter of attitudes and the acquiring of tools for further progress.[10] He will also have more time for the other problems of English teaching, especially for those of the larger matters of communication. When, however, there are differences of practice in the speech habits of his pupils, the principles that have been developed above in Chapters II, III, and IV should furnish the basis of determining what matters really deserve attention and what can be safely ignored.

Thus far we have spoken of language as a set of

[10] These will be the subjects of discussion in the next two chapters.

habits; we must now recognize the fact that language habits are of two distinct kinds. There are first the patterns or molds of the language or the particular dialect. "A language would be a difficult thing to handle if its speakers had the burden imposed on them of remembering every little item separately." [11] In the matter of forms there is, for example, the pattern by which modern English indicates plural number in nouns—the so-called -s ending. In learning the language the child hears so many words made to refer to more than one unit by the addition of this -s ending that he soon, although unconsciously, masters the pattern. When, then, he later says *three books* or *many toys,* neither he nor anyone else can know whether he has before heard these particular words in the plural forms or whether he is just then creating them for himself according to the pattern. If he says *three mans* or *two tooths* it is most likely that he is not repeating forms he has heard but is fitting new language material into the molds he knows. In like fashion the child soon learns the process of indicating past time in action words by means of the addition of a dental suffix. He may or may not have heard the past tense form of any particular word, *walked, called, talked,* but he creates them naturally according to the pattern he

[11] Otto Jespersen, *Philosophy of Grammar,* p. 21. See also his whole discussion of "Formulas and Free Expressions."

has learned. Such creation accounts for his use of forms like *runned, hitted, knowed, drawed.*

We have these patterns or molds in all parts of language,—in pronunciation and in the word order of sentences as well as in matters of morphology.

"The sentence he thus creates may, or may not, be different in some one or more respects from anything he has ever heard or uttered before; that is of no importance for our inquiry. What is essential is that in pronouncing it he conforms to a certain pattern. No matter what words he inserts, he builds up the sentence in the same way, and even without any special grammatical training we feel that the two sentences

John gave Mary the apple,
My uncle lent the joiner five shillings,

are analogous; that is, they are made after the same pattern. In both we have the same type. The words that make up the sentences are variable, but the type is fixed." [12]

Of the two kinds of speech habits, the second type consists of those special forms which do not conform to the usual patterns. Very frequently they are remnants of older patterns which no longer live in modern English. Thus the plurals *oxen* and *men* are special forms inherited from the older stages of the English language when a large number of words

[12] Otto Jespersen, *Philosophy of Grammar,* p. 19.

fitted into these particular patterns. Today most of them have been changed to conform to the -*s* pattern, leaving only a few isolated cases behind which the child must learn by frequent hearing and repeated use. In some cases like the past tense forms of verbs like *ride,* or *know,* or *sing* there is still left some feeling for the older patterns to which these verbs conformed, although most of the verbs which formerly followed these old patterns have now adjusted themselves to the mold of the dental suffix. *Glide, writhe, whine,* originally belonged with *ride;* and *crow, flow, mow, sow,* with *know.* "Vulgar" English with its greater conservatism is likely to feel the pull of these older patterns more than other dialects. It is the feeling for the pattern in such verbs as *sing* that accounts for *brang* and *brung.* Exceptional forms can only be maintained against the pull of the major patterns of modern English by their frequent repetitions in constant use.

In the English teacher's attempt to analyze the particular speech habits of the pupils of his class in preparation for a program of language teaching it is absolutely necessary that the two kinds of habits here discriminated be recognized and separately dealt with. At times there are new patterns or molds which must be established; at times the pull of old patterns must be broken; and at other times there are special forms which must replace those that have conformed to a pattern with which the dialect of the socially acceptable group does not yet associate it. Adequate diagnosis must precede any thoroughgoing attempt to develop in our pupils new speech habits.

Equally important with the question of what speech habits the schools should strive to develop is the problem of a sound procedure in the process of developing those habits. We must at all times realize that the process of mastering the speech habits of any social dialect of English which differs from the one to which we have been accustomed has much in common with learning a foreign language. English teachers can, therefore, profit from the studies made during recent years of methods of foreign language teaching. There are, however, four principles which from our knowledge of language processes seem valid guides for the developing of new speech habits in our pupils:

(1) There should be much *hearing* of the speech forms which constitute the habits to be adopted. The pupil should hear the desired forms repeatedly in all sorts of *normal* situations in which they ordinarily occur. Occasions for the pupil's use of the forms should follow, not precede, this becoming accustomed to their sound.

(2) The occasions provided for the pupil's exer-

cise of the desired habits must be essentially normal speech situations. Such practice should never be disconnected words nor even disconnected sentences. The context of a complete language situation is necessary to establishing the associative bases of the desired speech habits. In the earlier grades carefully devised language games can be employed; for the high school informal discussions of problems of interest to the students may furnish the desired practice in context. In this connection we must again insist that the language habits of spoken English must be developed in oral speech; that those of written English should be practiced in connection with writing.

(3) New language habits cannot be acquired in large doses. Our teaching becomes ineffective whenever the pupil is bewildered. One essential of progress, therefore, will be a carefully graded program of habit development which centers attention upon only a very few new matters at any one time but demands that the student carry forward and continually use all that he has learned. Such a program, based upon a scientific analysis of the speech habits of any particular dialect of the English language, has, I think, seldom been attempted in our schools.

(4) The measure of success in the developing of such new speech habits must be a test in which the

habits can function when the attention of the pupil is given wholly to meaning and not to language forms.

The most important factor in any successful teaching of language habits, especially in the high school and later, is the *pupil's will to learn the new dialect.* If he remains unconvinced that the new habits are really desirable the task is practically hopeless. The problem, therefore, of establishing desirable attitudes toward the language is the one that is fundamental. To it the next chapter will be devoted.

SELECTED REFERENCES

BAHLSON, LEOPOLD, *The Teaching of Modern Languages*, Chapters I, II, III, IV.

BLOOMFIELD, LEONARD, *The Study of Language*, pp. 223, 224, and Chapter IX.

BODE, B. H., *Modern Educational Theories*, Chap. IX.

BROWN, ROLLO W., *How the French Boy Learns to Write*, Chapters I, II, III, IV.

CARPENTER, BAKER, and SCOTT, *The Teaching of English*, pp. 52-66.

CHARTERS, W. W., *Minimal Essentials in English Language and Grammar*, Part I of the *Sixteenth Yearbook of the National Society for the Study of Education*, pp. 85-110.

DEWEY, JOHN, *How We Think*, Chapter XIII.

HOYT, FRANKLIN S., *The Place of Grammar in the Ele-*

mentary Curriculum, in *Teachers College Record,* Vol.
    VII, pp. 467-494.
JESPERSEN, OTTO, *How to Teach a Foreign Language.*
JESPERSEN, OTTO, *Language,* Chapters V, VI, VII.
JESPERSEN, OTTO, *Philosophy of Grammar,* Chapter I.
KRAPP, G. P., *Standards of Speech and Their Values,* in
    Mod. Phil., XI, pp. 57-70.
JOHNSON, ROY I., *The Persistency of Error in English
    Composition,* in *School Review,* XXV, pp. 555-580.
LEONARD, S. A., *English Composition as a Social Prob-
    lem,* Chapter IV.
LEONARD and MOFFAT, *Levels in English Usage,* in *Eng-
    lish Journal,* Vol. XVI, pp. 345-359.
LYMAN, R. L., *Fluency, Accuracy, and General Excel-
    lence in English Composition,* in *School Review,* Vol.
    XXVI, pp. 85-100.
PALMER, HAROLD E., *The Principles of Language Study.*
THORNDIKE, E. L., *The Teacher's Word Book.*
THORNDIKE, E. L., and OTHERS, *An Inventory of English
    Constructions with Measures of Their Importance,* in
    Teachers College Record, Vol. XXVIII, pp. 580-610.
SWEET, HENRY, *The Practical Study of Languages.*
STORMZAND and O'SHEA, *How Much English Grammar?*
Preliminary Report of the Grammar Subcommittee,
    English Journal, Vol. VIII, pp. 179-189.
The Teaching of English in England, pp. 57-71 and 278-
    294.

CHAPTER VII

THE PROBLEMS OF THE TEACHER: DEVELOPING ATTITUDES

IF, at this point, one thinks back to our description of the qualities of good or artistic English, he may feel that our discussion of language habits has led us into some contradictions. We formerly insisted that beauty of language, good or artistic English, does not consist in an external conformity with any set of language habits, that it does not rest in sounds or syllables or any particular language forms, that it is not a matter of pronunciation, nor of grammar, nor of vocabulary as such, but that it is to be measured by the fulness of realization which attends the language symbols used. And then, although we accepted this statement as a formulation of the final aim or objective in the teaching of the English language, we have, in the preceding chapter, just stressed the desirability of having the schools develop in the pupils the habits of speech which represent the practice of those who belong to the group we have called the socially acceptable. There is, however, but a seeming contradiction here. Fulness of realization in the process of communication demands language symbols that thoroughly fit, that are entirely familiar, that do not call attention to themselves by being peculiar, and that do not suggest users whose experience lies to any great extent outside the contacts of our group. To use in connection with the carrying on of the affairs of our communities a set of speech habits alien to those customarily used causes friction in communication—if not because of real misunderstanding, at least because of suggesting social contacts unusual in such situations. From a practical point of view, therefore, the mastery of the speech habits of the socially acceptable group is indeed a step toward attaining the goal of good English for those who are placed in situations where this dialect is customary.

Probably the most important reason why the schools have not usually been successful in teaching new language habits lies in the fact that the particular habits they have attempted to teach have had little relation to real life. School-mastered English has been something never heard in the active affairs of life; it has not been the language of any group heard and admired by the students. As an unusual language, its forms attracted attention to themselves; they suggested the schoolroom and rule books, and because of this friction in their use they failed to measure up to the standards of a practical good English. As long as the language forms we try to teach in the schools are those of an essentially artificial English unrelated to actual living expression, we cannot hope for any great success in arousing within our pupils the interest and purposing which is necessary to mastering new language habits. If, however, the dialect, the speech habits we set out to develop are really related to life, if they are indeed the practice of the group carrying on the affairs of English-speaking people, we can convince our pupils that the effort is worth while and can reasonably expect to establish the attitudes that will motivate that effort.

We can, however, hardly hope to be entirely successful in inspiring these attitudes by some of the methods commonly employed in schools. There is, for example, the common practice of penalizing the student who does not strive to use the speech habits demanded. His English credit is lowered whenever a forbidden expression appears in his speech or in his written papers. Often with the cooperation of the teachers of other subjects the pupil's grade in any study can be reduced if the language of his recitation in that study lapses into the unacceptable speech forms. This method is akin to the practice of marking a theme a failure if it contains three misspelled words. It attempts to motivate an external conformity by means of fear and despite the fact that teachers often report it useful in securing immediate results it seems psychologically unsound and incapable of developing the permanent attitudes necessary to attaining our goal. The fundamental difficulty in this method lies in the fact that the pupil has no thorough understanding of what it is all about or of any ultimate end to be attained. As a result he outwardly conforms only in so far as he finds it necessary to escape penalizing, and he has no motive for further effort whenever this particular pressure is removed.

Another common practice is the attempt to make the penalizing of credit in the school the symbol of a social penalizing of those who fail to use the speech habits demanded. Here the teachers strive to make the pupils understand the reasons for the pressure brought to bear upon them in the school and endeavor to have the pupils adopt those reasons as their own. As frequently presented to the pupils, those reasons consist in the statements that adult society judges a person's education by the language he uses, and that unless he habitually employs the prescribed speech forms he is at once marked as socially unfit and is discriminated against in the matter of opportunity. There is no doubt that this attempt to motivate the mastery of certain speech habits is essentially more sound than the one described above, in which the grade-book is wielded as a whip. Those reasons, as frequently given, however, have proved unconvincing to the pupils who refused to accept without question the teacher's declarations for the facts. These pupils have found that the particular prescribed speech forms were really useful only in the schoolroom and that there were many persons in positions of dignity and respect who used the language habits frowned upon by the teachers. This social pressure motive has thus not been very successful because the kind of social pressure appealed to by the teacher has been an imaginary, not a real one. We may at least say that whatever social pressure existed has not definitely supported the kind of school-mastered speech which the teachers advocated.

The social pressure motive, however, can be made an effective means of stimulating the mastery of new speech habits providing it is thoroughly understood by the pupil and its use in connection with the particular speech habits in question can be observed and verified by him. For his understanding he must realize language as not simply a set of signals for the communication of definite meanings but as a manner or behavior which suggests the character and attitude of the speaker as well. He must know that the people with whom he is daily coming in contact do continually attempt to estimate and judge his worth and for that purpose will utilize every type of evidence upon which any sort of conclusion can rest—his clothes, his cleanliness, his posture, his walk, his manners, his speech. Whether right or wrong, it is true that many believe that the speech habits will suggest more concerning the real character of a person than any other one type of behavior. Out of such knowledge the pupil can be brought to realize the social importance of first impressions and the handicap of speech habits that are really not those of the group we have called the socially acceptable.

We are here, however, trespassing upon our positive statements concerning the development of attitudes. The following sentences from John Dewey will provide a starting point for the expression of our view:

" . . . little can be accomplished by setting up 'interest' as an end or a method by itself. Interest is obtained not by thinking about it and consciously aiming at it, *but by considering and aiming at the conditions* that lie back of it, and compel it." [1]

Fundamental among the conditions determining *interest* in language and the first of the attitudes we desire is an understanding of the nature of language

[1] John Dewey, *Interest and Effort in Education*, p. 95.

and the significance of language differences. The pupil must be led to understand that language is not, as it sometimes appears from the treatments in our grammars, a logical system of rules nor is it a mass of arbitrary and unrelated facts. He must come to know it as a growing and developing medium of expression that has had a long history. If attention is centered on the changes now in progress, changes which he can observe in the actual speech of the community about him, it is possible not only to make him feel that language is now alive but also to prepare the way for an understanding interest in the language changes of the past. Some of the materials of the history of our language —some of the processes of vocabulary development, for example—can thus be given early in the high school course as a first step toward building the conditions out of which can come the view of language as a growing, living thing.

Out of such a view should come also a sense for the importance of usage and a growing habit of observing usage. Such observation, however, must soon lead to the recognition of the differences of practice in pronunciation, in vocabulary, and even in grammar. This recognition will not only provide the opportunity for a further investigation of the differences that exist in regional dialects and in class groups but it will also necessitate a growing understanding of the significance of differing speech habits. Upon such an understanding there is reasonable hope of motivating the student to acquire whatever speech habits are essential to adapting himself to the language of the socially acceptable group.

If, however, we are really to succeed in leading the pupil toward the goal we have defined above under the name of artistic language we must in some way arouse in him a compelling desire for *effective speech*. Our frequent assumption that this is a difficult if not impossible task seems, from experience, entirely untrue. As a matter of fact, the excessive use of slang by students is unmistakable evidence of a passion for vigorous expression already existing. Of course the expression is crude and the slang may offend our sensibilities, but the *motive*, the *attitude*, the *desire* is already born, is often quite vigorous in fact, and needs only careful stimulation and guidance. Too often, I am afraid, our efforts to eliminate all slang and our emphasis upon an external conformity with certain language forms kill the motive which it should be our primary aim to cultivate. We are so much concerned about *correctness* of form and are so thoroughly occupied in pruning the pupil's language in accord with our standards of *propriety* that we give all our attention to the cultivation of the negative virtues without regard to the effect of our labors upon his natural reaching out after vigorous, racy expression. It is in language as it is in the case of independent thinking on the part of the pupil. As teachers we are so much concerned that the pupil think the right things, that is, that he agree with the commonly accepted views, that by opposing every effort which would lead away from the beaten path we soon kill or drive under cover whatever intellectual curiosity is still active.

More than that, we often fail to recognize that any development of the pupil's motives and desires for an effective use of language must begin on his own level. His growing power must function satisfactorily in his present communications with his own companions—those with whom he is now in daily contact. We cannot expect to develop a vivid and keen desire for what we tell him will be the kind of language to serve as a preparation for communication with some group of adults with whom he may in the future come into contact. In other words, if we would sensitize our pupils to effective English we must develop that sensitiveness in the social language situations that now exist for them. They can be led to realize the significance of finely adapting their language to the demands of ideas, occasions, and hearers only through their actual contacts with particular hearers on specific occasions.

We cannot possibly give them samples of all kinds of occasions and every class of hearers and it is doubtful if such a procedure would serve to develop the power we seek. We can, however, make them sensitive to the demands of the particular groups that *normally surround them* and that attitude is of far greater importance in their progress toward effective speech than any specific speech habits.

In this chapter we have thus far insisted that in general the desirable attitudes in language matters must rest upon and grow out of an adequate understanding and knowledge. Specifically we have urged: (1) that the desire and will to master particular speech habits must have its roots in an understanding of the life and growth of language and a realization of the social meaning and effect of differing sets of language patterns and forms; (2) that the desire for vigorous expression is already alive in most of our students but is thwarted by the usual procedure of language training which magnifies *propriety* and *correctness;* (3) that the sensitiveness to the particular demands of various situations necessitating communication can be developed best on the level at which the student now stands and in connection with the contacts now normal to him.

One other matter needs consideration here.

"It does not suffice to arouse energy; the *course*

that energy takes, the results that it effects, are the important matters." [2]

With the emphasis that has here been placed upon energy and vigor in the matter of expression and the protest against the methods that result in the usual curbing and checking of that energy one is likely to conclude that every interference with the realization of the pupil's desire for a racy, effective speech is to be condemned. There is no question that so much of our attention has hitherto been devoted to the curbing and pruning process that we must continually and strongly insist that our first problem is always the stimulating of this motive to force and vigor. But our task in the developing of attitudes is by no means accomplished if we fail to set up with our pupils ideals of good English which can be made thoroughly sound principles to guide the development of their language ability. The phrase, "to set up *with* our pupils," is here used deliberately to indicate a definite procedure. These ideals of good English cannot be set up *for* the pupils. If they are to become effective guides in the pupils' language development they must result from an inductive process. An appreciation of a vigorous and telling piece of slang here, of a racy comment there, of an especially fitting phrasing of an inter-

[3] John Dewey, *Interest and Effort in Education,* p. 91.

esting idea in another place, of the flatness and futility of one retort and the bad taste of another, such an appreciation stimulated day after day and week after week will grow naturally into ideals of good English possessing the power essential to directing the pupils' choice of language material.

In this process there is danger in hurry. Very frequently our eyes are fixed too closely upon the end to be attained and we strive for immediate results that can be measured at once. Such immediate results we obtain but often at the expense of the pupil's power to go on growing. If we would have him prepared for unlimited growth we cannot stress too much the fundamental necessity of the desirable attitudes in language matters and an equipment of tools which he can use without the direct guidance of the teacher.

SELECTED REFERENCES

Academy Papers, Addresses on Language Problems by Members of the American Academy of Arts and Letters, (Scribners, 1925).

BLOOMFIELD, LEONARD, *The Study of Language*, Chapter X.

BROWN, ROLLO W., *How the French Boy Learns to Write*, Chapter VIII.

Century Dictionary, Preface, Vol. I.

COAN, MARION S., *Historical Grammar in the High*

School, in Teachers College Record, Vol. VII, pp. 501-511.

DEWEY, JOHN, *Interest and Effort in Education.*

HOLLINGSWORTH, H. L., *The Psychology of Thought,* Chapter XV.

JESPERSON, OTTO, *The Teaching of Grammar,* in *English Journal,* Vol. XIII, pp. 161-176.

KENYON, J. S., *American Pronunciation,* pp. 3-7.

KILPATRICK, W. H., *Foundations of Method,* Chapters X, XI, XII.

LEONARD and COX, *General Language.*

LOUNSBURY, T. R., *The Standard of Usage in English,* Chapter V.

New English Dictionary, Preface, Volume I.

PALMER, H. E., *The Principles of Language Study,* Chap. XIII.

Reorganization of English in the Secondary School, Chapter X.

SCOTT and CARR, *The Development of Language.*

THOMA, WILHELMINA, *The Making of the English Language.*

THOMA, WILHELMINA, *Language Study in the High School,* in *English Journal,* Vol. XII, pp. 404-406.

Webster's New International Dictionary, Preface.

CHAPTER VIII

The Problems of the Teacher: Acquiring Tools

"Every teacher a teacher of English" is a slogan that finds a place in many of the writings on the teaching of English. Some school systems conscientiously attempt to practice the suggestion. At least there is the effort to make the students use in all recitations the particular habits which the English teacher is striving to develop. Even with thorough coöperation, however, we are driven to the conclusion that the time is all too short to accomplish what should be done in respect to the mastery of satisfactory English. We simply cannot hope to turn out our pupils equipped with a developed ability to use *good English* [1] upon every occasion. We cannot be charged with failure because we cannot accomplish the impossible. We do fail, however, if our pupils are not provided in the schools with the means of further growing after they leave our

---

[1] This phrase, *good English*, is of course to be understood in accord with the definition given above in Chapter V.

guidance. In the matter of the English language the motives and desires which can be developed within the school will furnish the dynamic of further growth if we can give our pupils the tools to make that growth possible. Such an equipment of attitudes and tools will make possible a much greater progress toward our ideal of good English than any number of specific habits we could possibly inculcate even if we had at our disposal the pupil's entire school time.

These tools can be rather definitely enumerated. First there are those to enable the student to observe, record, and analyze pronunciation.

"It is not sufficient merely to correct the various errors of pronunciation as they occur, or to insist on the children 'speaking out.' They should learn to recognize every sound in standard English, should observe for themselves how sounds are produced and modified by the position of the speech organs, and should practice producing them properly. The really scientific method, of course, would be to associate each sound with a phonetic symbol. This may seem to some teachers an alarming suggestion, but the learning of the symbols will be found a very simple matter both by teachers and children, and the teacher needs some means, which our system of spelling unfortunately does not afford, of referring to the sounds of the spoken language without actually producing them." [2]

There are here suggested two tools as extremely valuable if not absolutely indispensable aids to the development of ability to deal with pronunciation. First, the report just quoted urges a phonetic alphabet. All agree that we must have some system of symbols to indicate the sounds of our language and to record the pronunciation of words. All agree, too, that the conventional spelling alone will not be sufficient. The only question upon which there is a real difference of opinion concerns the relative merits of the phonetic alphabet [3] and a system of diacritical marks. The two systems differ fundamentally in principle, not simply in respect to convenience. Diacritical marks are symbols applied to the letters used in spelling a word and thus they center attention upon and emphasize the conven-

[2] *The Teaching of English in England* (Government report), pp. 65, 66.

[3] I have here used the expression "the phonetic alphabet" as if there were but one. Such an assumption a generation or even a decade ago would have been indefensible for there were many systems of phonetic notation with no one alphabet very distinctly favored. Today it seems fair to say that among language scholars generally the notation of the International Phonetic Association is so widely accepted and used that it can fairly be called "the phonetic alphabet." Present differences in practice are usually in the nature of modifications and simplifications of that alphabet.

tional spelling. Similarity of sounds when represented by different letters is entirely ignored. Thus in the system of diacritical marks used in *Webster's New International Dictionary* [4] there are ten different marks to indicate the various sounds represented by the letter *a*. (ā, ȧ, ă, ȧ, â, ä, à, á, a̜, a̤.) There are nine marks to indicate the various sounds of the letter *o*. (ō, ô, ŏ, ŏ, ô, ŏ, ó, o̜, o̤). Similarities of the vowel sounds in *what* and *odd* are ignored and obscured because the first is marked as a sound of *a* and the second as a sound of *o*. Such similarities of vowel sound are also obscured in groups of words like the following: *wolf, full, foot; there, care; food, do, rude.*

A phonetic notation, however, is in principle, an attempt to represent each sound of the language by a separate symbol and by one symbol only. It emphasizes and centers attention upon the sounds used in the pronunciation of words and ignores the spelling. Thus the vowel sound in the word *me* is always indicated by the symbol [i] no matter how it

---

[4] In this discussion I am quoting from the *Chart of English Sounds, as Represented in Webster's New International Dictionary,* published by G. & C. Merriam Company. I am using the "symbols which may be used in marking words without respelling." It is to be noted that whenever we respell words to indicate their pronunciation we *are using in principle a phonetic notation*. In the current edition of *Webster's New International Dictionary* many words are thus respelled. This dictionary has, therefore, been abandoning a purely diacritical system and moving toward a phonetic alphabet.

happens to be represented in the conventional spelling of the words— *yield, machine, receive, people,
beat, beet.*

A system of diacritical marks does serve to support
the teaching of spelling but it is an exceedingly
difficult means of dealing with pronunciation. In
the Webster chart there are more than fifty symbols
for the representations of the different vowel sounds
and some thirty-eight for the consonant sounds. In
addition, if one tries to use these symbols to record
pronunciations heard he must always remember the
conventional spelling of the words before he can
apply the symbols to indicate the sounds used. On
the whole such a procedure will tend to develop
thoroughly wrong ideas about the nature of language. It will tend to strengthen the view that our
language is fundamentally something written and
that our words are *combinations of letters* rather
than lead to the attitude that language is primarily
sounds for which the written letters are merely in-
adequate representations.

On the other hand, a "broad" system of the
phonetic alphabet has many distinct advantages as
a tool for pupils. Forty symbols are sufficient to
indicate the important differences in the sounds of
our language. Of these forty all but ten are the
usual letters of our alphabet. Experiments with

children of the seventh, eighth, and ninth grades [5] show that these symbols can be more quickly and completely learned and more satisfactorily retained for use than the system of diacritical marks with respelling now used in *Webster's New International Dictionary*. The most important advantage of the learning and use of the phonetic alphabet, however, lies in the fact that it serves as a first step in developing a sound view of the nature of language and a desirable attitude toward linguistic phenomena.

The second tool which the report quoted above urges in respect to "speech training" is an elementary knowledge of phonetics.

"They should learn to recognize every sound in standard English, should observe for themselves how sounds are produced and modified by the position of the speech organs, and should practice producing them properly." [6]

Phonetics as the science of speech sounds is an extensive body of knowledge but some of the simple matters of that science can be understood by young pupils and used by them to advantage in observing

[5] The experiments referred to here are not yet finished and the statement is made upon incomplete returns. It seems justified, however, by the results already secured. We hope to publish soon in one of the educational journals a report of this work.

[6] *The Teaching of English in England,* p. 65.

more accurately their own pronunciation and that
of those about them. This is especially true of the
descriptions of the important sounds of the English
language in terms of the movements by which they
are produced. All through the grades and the high
school, teachers at times discuss pronunciation with
their pupils and often attempt to analyze our language sounds as well as to point out differences between them. Simple descriptions of such sounds in
accord with the methods of analysis which the
science of phonetics uses will furnish pupils with
clear and practically accurate statements instead
of the hazy and often absolutely wrong statements
now frequently used. We shall then speak no more
about "dropping the *g*'s" in pronouncing such words
as *reading* and *writing* for, to be accurate, the pronunciations which we designate by the spellings
readin' and *writin'* have *not dropped* any sound.
They have simply substituted tip-tongue nasals for
base-tongue nasals. In other words, in both cases
the air is allowed to continue through the nose, but
in *readin'* and *writin'* the oral passage is stopped by
the tip of the tongue whereas in *reading* and *writing*
the oral passage is stopped by the base of the tongue.
It will be easy likewise to describe the differences between the pronunciations of the initial sounds of
the words *pin, tin, kin,* or the differences between
the initial sounds of *thin, sin, shin,* in terms of the

places in the oral passage at which the stoppage or the friction occurs.

Such descriptions need not be intricate to be valuable. Minute discriminations are not for such pupils, and, for practical purposes, all differences can well be ignored which do not readily show themselves to function as distinguishing sounds of our language. There is, however, no better way to introduce pupils to the essential nature of language and to develop in them an enlightened judgment in questions of pronunciation than to help them to acquire some of the elementary matters of phonetics as a tool.[7]

Besides these tools that have their use in dealing with pronunciation there are, next, those which are necessary to understanding the structure of English sentences. At once we are plunged into the controversy concerning the value of a study of English grammar. There are those who vigorously insist that a study of grammar

"(a) fails to provide a general mental training,

[7] Another value claimed for the elementary study of phonetics is set forth in the following quotation:

"Among the practical uses of phonetics is to be mentioned its effect is stimulating good articulation. Familiar knowledge and daily observation of the manner in which the sounds of speech are made with the speech organs develops an habitual consciousness of the operation of those organs in daily speech that results in improved articulation."

J. S. Kenyon, *American Pronunciation*, p. 6.

ACQUIRING TOOLS

169

(b) does not enable the teachers to eradicate solecisms, (c) does not aid in composition, and (d) takes up time which could more profitably be devoted to the study of literature." [8]

These views seem also to be supported by the results of the few measured experiments that are available. According to such investigations there appears to be no correlation between a knowledge of English grammar and correct speaking and writing.[9] On the other hand there are those of equal experience and authority who assert with even more vigor that "immense harm has been done by the well-meant discouragement of formal grammar in the elementary schools" [10] and deplore the fact that even our best pupils are often "quite at sea on simple principles of sentence structure which are vital to all linguistic study."

These opposing views concerning the value of the study of English grammar seem to me to arise from the facts (1) that the parties to the controversy do

[8] *The Teaching of English in England,* p. 279, quoting Dr. P. B. Ballard. He has since developed this thesis in a book entitled *Teaching the Mother Tongue.*

[9] Franklin S. Hoyt, *Grammar in the Elementary Curriculum,* in *Teachers College Record,* Vol. VII, pp. 467-499.

(p. 485) "A comparison of the correlations obtained . . . will show that, in so far as the results are trustworthy, there is about the same relationship existing between grammar and composition and grammar and interpretation, as exists between any two totally different subjects, as grammar and geography."

[10] *The Teaching of English in England,* p. 278, quoting Mr. J. E. Barton.

not use the term *grammar* to cover the same material and (2) that they are by no means agreed as to the purpose of grammar study. A clear definition, therefore, as to both these points ought not only to aid in resolving the dispute but also to serve as a description of the tools which pupils need in dealing with the structure of sentences. The two quotations following illustrate two opposing views of the nature and purpose of the study of grammar. The first expresses the attitude commonly held in the schools and repudiated earlier in this book;[11] the second is in accord with the scientific point of view.

"Grammar consists of a series of rules and definitions. . . . The difference between the purpose in teaching language and that of teaching grammar is this: In language when we correct grammatical forms we merely teach the correct form, while in grammar we explain why it is correct. . . . Since, however, ninety-five per cent of all children and teachers come from homes or communities where incorrect English is used, nearly everyone has before him the long, hard task of overcoming habits set up early in life before he studied language and grammar in school. . . . Such people are exposed to the ridicule of those who notice the error, and the only way in which they can cure themselves is by eternal vigilance and the study of grammar." [12]

[11] See Chapters I and II.

[12] W. W. Charters, *Teaching the Common Branches* (Revised and enlarged edition, 1924), pp. 115, 96, 98.

"It is quite a mistaken idea to suppose that English grammars are written to teach English people how to speak their own language. Men who write grammars do not suppose that they can set up a model of English speech, however much they may wish to do so. Hardly anyone, as a matter of fact, alters his way of speaking because a Grammar tells him that his way is wrong, or that another way is right. This would indeed be putting the cart before the horse. A Grammar book does _not_ attempt to teach people how they _ought_ to speak, but on the contrary, unless it is a very bad or a very old work, it merely states how, as a matter of fact, certain people do speak at the time at which it is written." [13]

The study of grammar, therefore, finds its purpose in providing the pupils not with "the rules of correct English" but with (1) an apparatus by which to analyze the logical relations of words and word groups within the speech unit we call the sentence, and (2) a description of the means which the English language uses to express grammatical ideas and relationships.[14]

"Every language can and must express the fundamental syntactic relations even though there is not a single affix to be found in its vocabulary." [15]

[13] H. C. Wyld, *Elementary Lessons in English Grammar*, pp. 11, 12.

[14] See the type of grammar indicated above in Chapter II, p. 44.

[15] Edward Sapir, *Language*, p. 132.

The pupil must learn, therefore, what "these fundamental syntactic relations" are in order that he may have an apparatus for analyzing the structure of the thoughts which sentences express. If, also, we would have him observe intelligently the facts of the language usage about him he must become thoroughly familiar with the three types of devices which our particular language uses to indicate not only these syntactic relations but other grammatical ideas as well. To be more definite, he must know the usual grammatical uses in English of word forms or inflections, of function words, and of word order. It is in these respects that the various sets of language habits differ and only in so far as the pupil can thus refer any given usage to the pattern has he the tools necessary to make intelligent observations and decisions for himself.

Finally, in addition to the tools necessary to observe, record, and analyze pronunciation, and those which are essential to observing and understanding the grammar of our language, there are the tools which will provide the equipment for dealing intelligently with matters of vocabulary. Fashions in words, their uses and their meanings, change more rapidly, at least more noticeably, than either sounds or grammar, so that in matters of vocabulary more than elsewhere there is need for an appreciation of language as a living, developing, changing medium of communication. An elementary knowledge of the processes of vocabulary growth is within the range of grasp of rather young pupils and ought, perhaps, to be the most important outcome of the dictionary work commonly given in the junior high school.

These processes include, first, the ways by which the internal resources of the vocabulary are developed. One of the most important is "composition"—the joining of two words to form a third with a specialized meaning other than that of the two words taken separately. (*Railroad, broadcast, typewriter, telephone, policeman.*) Another is "functional change"—the use of a word in a grammatical situation other than the one in which it is usually employed. (To *stone* a cat, to *brown* the toast, a *feed*, a *choice* melon.) Still another is "metaphorical change"—the use of a word to indicate a figurative comparison: (The *brow* of a precipice, throw *light* upon a problem, a *harrowing* episode). These, as well as the methods by which slang is created, have been discussed to some extent above.[16] They are enumerated here in order to point out the kind of processes one should understand in order to interpret the changes now affecting the words of our vocabulary.

In addition to these methods of development,

[16] Chapter IV.

English has for centuries been hospitable to foreign words. To build up inductively conceptions of the great periods of borrowing, of the present conglomerate nature of the vocabulary, of the kinds of words taken in and the reasons for their assimilation, of the various degrees to which they have been naturalized, of the resulting different levels of discourse— to build up conceptions of these facts from a study of our words by the use of the dictionary will not only serve to aid pupils to grasp the nature and processes of language but will also provide them with tools that may be used in trying to adapt their language nicely to the demands of varied situations.

One need not, of course, call attention to the fact that acquiring the tools of language study will never in itself accomplish any good results. Unless acquiring the tools is joined with the will to understand language or the keen desire to master effective expression they are of very little value. Indeed, it is only as such a will and desire motivates the acquiring of the tools that they can be satisfactorily mastered for real use. On the other hand, the will to attain real power of expression, the attitudes which we have discussed in the preceding chapter, must necessarily be thwarted unless the tools can be acquired to make possible continued development through intelligent observation of language practice.

SELECTED REFERENCES

BLOOMFIELD, LEONARD, *The Study of Language*, Chapter II.

DEWEY, JOHN, *How We Think*, Chapter XIV.

FRIES, C. C., *An Introduction to Modern English Grammar*, (to be published soon).

GRATTAN and GURREY, *Our Living Language*.

GREENOUGH and KITTREDGE, *Words and Their Ways in English Speech*.

JESPERSEN, OTTO, *How to Teach a Foreign Language*, Chapter X.

JESPERSON, OTTO, *The Teaching of Grammar*, in *The English Journal*, Vol. XIII, pp. 161-176. (Mar. 1925).

KENYON, J. S., *American Pronunciation*.

KRAPP, G. P., *The Pronunciation of Standard English in America*.

The Teaching of English in England, Chapters III, IV, IX.

CHAPTER IX

The Equipment of the Teacher of the English Language

If the program for the teaching of the English language here set forth is sound in general, then it is obvious that the teacher of English must know more about that language than has usually been the case hitherto. We can no longer tolerate the view that anyone who speaks and writes English with fair success is prepared to teach the English language in the schools. Even in the junior high school the pupils come with at least ten years of experience in speaking English and with five years of reading and writing it. The teacher of English must be prepared to diagnose whatever difficulties may attend their use of language at this stage and to lead on in their development of knowledge and power.

Nor can one assume that much work in the field of literature or even many courses in rhetoric and composition will necessarily provide an adequate training to teach the English language. One may be very well trained in these aspects of the field called "English" and yet hopelessly incompetent to deal with language matters. In this chapter we are concerned only with the special equipment necessary to the teacher of English language.

One should like to ignore the demands of the practical situation and outline here for the teacher such a training as would really enable him to be an independent practitioner in a true profession. With the present conditions, however, such a training for the rank and file of English teachers is entirely out of the question. Certainly with the present salaries paid by school boards the investment of enough capital to enable one to attain it would be economically unprofitable. We must, therefore, attempt to state the mere essentials of an equipment which will enable the English teacher to maintain his bearings in the field of English language and provide the tools which will assist him to find solutions for most of the practical problems with which he will be confronted.

In matters of pronunciation a teacher without a knowledge of phonetics is as useless as a physician who knows no anatomy.

"A serious aspect of this general lack of knowledge of the simplest phonetic facts of our own language, is that many school-teachers have wrong habits of speech, usually artificially acquired, and they unintentionally mislead their pupils in pronunciation. This is to be deplored, not as a matter of blame to the teachers, but as a serious defect in an educational system which fails to provide and require the necessary preparation of the teacher. Realizing this defect, the Board of Education in England several years ago made phonetics a requirement in the preparation of elementary school teachers.

"To cite only a single instance of the present situation in our schools, the writer has repeatedly heard school-teachers insist on the full pronunciation of the vowel in the unaccented syllables of words —a rule which neither they nor their pupils can follow in natural, unconscious speech. One city teacher of high standing drilled her pupils carefully to pronounce the noun *subject* with the full sound of the *e* as in *let,* and in the same recitation, after passing to another topic, herself repeatedly pronounced the same word naturally, would obscure *e* [ɪ], as anyone properly should do. The author has observed scores of similar instances of false teaching in the pronunciation of teachers otherwise well prepared and devoted to their work." [1]

It is of course impossible to expect all teachers of English to be so thoroughly trained in phonetics that they could without special aid deal with all the problems of enunciation and pronunciation that may arise. It is to be hoped that the day is not far off when school administrators will become convinced

[1] J. S. Kenyon, *American Pronunciation,* p. 4.

that at least one specialist in speech, thoroughly and scientifically trained, is as necessary to a school system as specialists in music, or in drawing, or in health. Teachers need very greatly the services of such a specialist, one to whom they could go for guidance and to whom they could refer difficult problems. All that we can at present look for in the classroom teacher is such an elementary knowledge of phonetics as will enable him to recognize the real nature of the problems before him and will open for him the sources of scholarly information. The scientific books on matters of pronunciation are closed to those who do not understand the terminology and the symbols used. The classroom teacher should at least have available and be able to use standard books of reference in spite of their somewhat technical treatment.

In matters of English language other than pronunciation the problem of the teacher's equipment is even more difficult. The scientific point of view rests upon the historical method. The problems arising in the present state of English in America cannot be satisfactorily appreciated unless viewed in the light of the history of the language. Obviously, then, the teacher of the English language should not only know the earlier stages of English but should have so assimilated this material in all its social bearings that he can readily evaluate the language practices of his pupils. But this must be a counsel of perfection or at least an ideal or objective toward which we should strive in the training of our teachers. As a matter of fact it is extremely doubtful whether any large number of the prospective teachers who do now take our regular college courses in Old English, in Middle English, in Historical Grammar ever arrive at such a familiarity with the development of our language and linguistic processes that they really can thus "readily evaluate the language practices of pupils." And all too frequently the blame is to be attributed in some large measure to the nature of the courses as they are now given and not entirely to the students who pursue them. The following paragraphs, coming as they do from a most excellent teacher of the English language, are significant.

"My experience leads me to suspect that no courses in English are more formalized and curriculum-inherited than the average course in the language of the older stages of our speech. They generally get no farther than the learning (sometimes not even that) of the forms and vocabulary of the older language, with some parallels between modern and older forms. . . . A broad language experience is seldom obtained from these courses.

"Courses in the English language were established and stabilized in American Universities forty or fifty years ago when the enthusiasm for the new study of earlier English was running high, and when we were beginning to learn of our ethnic relations through philological evidence. At that time there was much new to discovery in this field and the courses fitted the uppermost interest of that day. The general nature of the courses has remained practically unchanged and has failed to respond to newer language interests. They are frequently given to and demanded of graduate students largely through a blind faith that it is the thing to do. Beyond the woods of the inflectional forms students are not brought to see that the Old English we teach as a fundamental of scholarship in English and as a preparation for teaching modern English was a highly conventionalized written language, a cultivated learned dialect, practiced by only a few of the inhabitants of old England; that the political and social barriers which upheld it fell away with the Norman Conquest and that chaos reigned in language in the Middle English period, as it would reign today had we not the conservative influences of education, teaching, print, and a tremendously deep class-consciousness. I do not care particularly how deeply versed in the varieties of Middle English dialects a teacher may be or how much he has learned of Chaucer's sources or the authorship of 'Piers the Plowman'; unless he comes through a Middle English course with an appreciation of the startling likeness of the language conditions of that day and of this (with tremendous unlikenesses also), his course is in vain as a preparation for teaching the language today." [2]

On the other hand, one cannot entirely ignore the fact that many of the students in our language courses, prospective teachers of English language, become exceedingly impatient of the preliminary drudgery incident to mastering those facts and details that are essential to the building of a sound point of view and a rounded language experience. Concerning the history of the English language, therefore, in view of its importance for the problems of the teacher, it is not too much to demand that that teacher should have enough familiarity with the older stages of the language and the processes of sound change and analogy that have operated in its development to understand the nature of the difficulties arising in connection with the forms and syntax used by pupils.

More than everything else, however, the teacher of the English language needs a clear point of view based upon an adequate knowledge of the facts and well thought through. Under the present conditions it is not only difficult to attain such a clearly grasped view for oneself; it is especially hard to fulfill the duty of a missionary in behalf of that view as the teacher must. The public generally, both in Eng-

[2] J. F. Royster, *The Preparation of the English Teacher* in *The English Journal*, Vol. XII, pp. 402, 403.

land and in America, are interested, extremely interested, in matters concerning the language, but they are also extremely ignorant of all that pertains to the scientific view. With it all they are violent and intolerant, so that the missionary's task is by no means a peaceful one.

" . . . there is but slight evidence as yet that the Universities have made any impression, directly or indirectly, among the public at large, by disseminating sound knowledge concerning the history of the English tongue. Not that the public generally is uninterested in the subject. That is the tragedy of the situation. The public is extraordinarily interested in all sorts of questions connected with English Philology; in etymology, in varieties of pronunciation and grammatical usage, in the sources of the Cockney dialect, in vocabulary, in the origin of place and personal names, in the pronunciation of Chaucer and Shakespeare. You may hear these matters discussed in railway carriages and smoking-rooms; you may read long letters about them in the press, adorned sometimes with a display of curious information, collected at random, misunderstood, wrongly interpreted, and used in an absurd way to bolster up preposterous theories. No, the subject-matter of English Philology possesses a strange fascination for the man in the street, but almost everything that he thinks and says about it is incredibly and hopelessly wrong. There is no subject which attracts a larger number of cranks and quacks than

English Philology. In no subject, probably, is the knowledge of the educated public at a lower ebb. The general ignorance concerning it is so profound that it is very difficult to persuade people that there really is a considerable mass of well-ascertained fact, and a definite body of doctrine on linguistic questions." [3]

In his study and his thinking the teacher can afford to neglect neither the ultra-puristic attitude nor the extreme scientific view. It will not do for him to adopt either one or even a middle ground and ignore the others. He must know the opposing views as thoroughly as he masters the facts that support the one he adopts. In the present unsettled conditions he must realize that every point of view has its vigorous assailants and he must be prepared to defend his ground upon every side. More than that, to be a missionary equipped for real service he must know both the language and the thought of the people to whom he goes.

Especially tactful must the teacher be in dealing with the attitudes which have become traditional in the schools. Much school teaching still perpetuates the eighteenth-century attitude toward language, but there is a growing attempt to bring into

[3] H. C. Wyld, *English Philology in English Universities*, (An Inaugural Lecture, Feb. 2, 1921), p. 10.

the schools the views that arise out of the past hundred years of linguistic study based upon the scientific method. In the overthrow of the traditional view and the adjustments in teaching which must take place there is especial need for a clear-headed dealing with difficult problems. From a practical education point of view there is nothing to be gained and much to be lost by a fanatical endorsement and advocacy of either the traditional or the scientific claims. The local conditions must always determine the details of a practical program by which the principles here advocated can guide the teaching of the English language in the schools.

What has been said in urging tact, however, must not be taken to imply that there is no place for enthusiasm in advocating the newer views of language and language teaching. Indeed, one has most excellent reason for feeling confident that in this approach lies the great hope of giving life and vitality to the dry bones of grammar and its kin. Not only as a teacher but as student of his subject the teacher of the English language cannot fail to become enthusiastic if he catches a vision of the full possibilities of his field.

"Language as a whole, in all its aspects, its words and idioms, its coarseness and its reticences, its pronunciation, and the very tones of voice, language in its completeness, is the most perfect mirror of the manners of the age. . . .

"The invitation which a student of the history of a language utters to the companions of his voyage of discovery should be:

" 'Together let us beat this ample field,
Try what the open, what the covert yield;
The latent tracts, the giddy heights explore,
Of all who blindly creep, or sightless soar;
Eye nature's walks, shoot folly as it flies,
And catch the manners living as they rise.' " [4]

SELECTED REFERENCES

BROWN, ROLLO W., *How the French Boy Learns to Write*, Chapter VII.

CROSS, E. A., *Fundamentals in English.*

KENNEDY, ARTHUR G., *A Bibliography of Writings on the English Language from the Beginning of Printing to the End of 1922.*

PALMER, HAROLD E., *The Scientific Study and Teaching of Languages*, Part VII.

PRIOR, D. O., *The Place of Philology in the Training of the School Teacher*, in *Modern Language Teaching*, Vol. 14, pp. 45-54.

ROYSTER, J. F., *The Preparation of the English Teacher*, in *The English Journal*, Vol. XII, pp. 397-404.

WYLD, H. C., *The Neglect of the Study of the English Language in the Training of Teachers*, (University Press, Liverpool).

[4] H. C. Wyld, *History of Modern Colloquial English*, p. 24.

Bibliography of English Language and Literature, 1920—
for the Modern Humanities Research Association.

The Reorganization of English in the Secondary School,
bibliography on p. 174.

The Teaching of English in England, Chapter VI, pp.
167-194.

H